Social Work Leadership in Healthcare: Directors' Perspectives

Social Work Leadership in Healthcare: Directors' Perspectives

Gary Rosenberg, PhD
Andrew Weissman, DSW
Editors

Routledge
Taylor & Francis Group
New York   London

Social Work Leadership in Healthcare: Directors' Perspectives has also been published as *Social Work in Health Care*, Volume 20, Number 4 1995.

The development, preparation, and publication of this work has been undertaken with great care. However, the publisher, employees, editors, and agents of The Haworth Press and all imprints of The Haworth Press, Inc., including The Haworth Medical Press and Pharmaceutical Products Press, are not responsible for any errors contained herein or for consequences that may ensue from use of materials or information contained in this work. Opinions expressed by the author(s) are not necessarily those of The Haworth Press, Inc.

First published 1995 by The Haworth Press, Inc.

10 Alice Street, Binghamton, NY 13904-1580 USA

This edition published 2012 by Routledge

Routledge
Taylor & Francis Group
711 Third Avenue
New York, NY 10017

Routledge
Taylor & Francis Group
2 Park Square,
Milton Park, Abingdon,
Oxfordshire OX14 4RN

First issued in paperback 2016

Routledge is an imprint of the Taylor & Francis Group, an informa business

Library of Congress Cataloging-in-Publication Data

Social work leadership in healthcare : directors' perspectives / Gary Rosenberg, Andrew Weissman, editors.
      p. cm.
      Includes bibliographical references.
      ISBN 1-56024-764-9 (alk. paper)
      1. Medical social work–United States–Administration. 2. Social work administration–United States. 3. Health facilities–United States–Administration. I. Rosenberg, Gary. II. Weissman, Andrew, 1941-
HV687.5.U5S647 1995
362.1'0425–dc20   95-23135
                                                                   CIP

ISBN 13: 978-1-138-98236-9 (pbk)
ISBN 13: 978-1-56024-764-7 (hbk)

Social Work Leadership in Healthcare: Directors' Perspectives

CONTENTS

ABOUT THE EDITORS

Gary Rosenberg, PhD, is the Edith J. Baerwald Professor of Community Medicine (Social Work) and Senior Vice President at The Mount Sinai Medical Center, New York City. He is past President of the Society for Social Work Administrators in Health Care. Dr. Rosenberg has been elected to the Hunter College Hall of Fame and has received the Distinguished Alumni Award from Adelphi University and the Founders Day Award from New York University. In addition, he is a Fellow in the Brookdale Center on Aging, a Fellow in the New York Academy of Medicine, and a recipient of the Ida M. Cannon Award of the Society for Hospital Social Work Directors.

Andrew Weissman, DSW, is Assistant Professor in the Department of Community Medicine (Social Work) and an Administrator in the Office of the Senior Vice President at The Mount Sinai Medical Center, New York City. He is a past Director of the Department of Social Work Services of The Mount Sinai Hospital. He is also a recipient of the Ida M. Cannon Award of the Society of Social Work Directors of The American Hospital Association.

Introduction

Gary Rosenberg, PhD
Andrew Weissman, DSW

Effective Social Work Administrators in healthcare organizations introduce timely and significant program innovations and effectively manage social work services to families and individuals. These managers translate the professional service activities of social workers to other managers in the healthcare organization, link the healthcare organization to the community and speak to the broader issues of healthcare policy and legislation.

The purpose of this special volume of *Social Work in Health Care* is to provide a set of responses by a number of our colleagues to a changing healthcare environment and to provide us with models that help improve the social work services functions in healthcare organizations.

In the Spring of 1987 Gary Rosenberg and Sylvia Clarke edited a special volume of *Social Work in Health Care* called, "Social Workers in Healthcare Management: The Move to Leadership." At that time the questions raised concerned the mobility of Social Work Managers in the healthcare system: What were the nature of their conflicts? What were the ethical dilemmas they faced? What were the stresses involved in moving from the management of a resource service area to executive level management?

Today, social work services are faced with a transformation of the healthcare milieu. The hospital will not remain the hub of the healthcare system. In the move toward managed and capitated care

[Haworth co-indexing entry note]: "Introduction." Rosenberg, Gary, and Andrew Weissman. Co-published simultaneously in *Social Work in Health Care* (The Haworth Press, Inc.) Vol. 20, No. 4, 1995, pp. 1-2; and: *Social Work Leadership in Healthcare: Directors' Perspectives* (ed: Gary Rosenberg, and Andrew Weissman), The Haworth Press, Inc., 1995, pp. 1-2. Multiple copies of this article/chapter may be purchased from The Haworth Document Delivery Center [1-800-3-HAWORTH; 9:00 a.m. - 5:00 p.m. (EST)].

social work and other departments are being decentralized. Social work directors are assuming programmatic operational positions in the healthcare arena.

How can social work plan to meet the challenges we face today and in the future? How can social work skills and values help maintain the meeting of common human needs by complex health care organizations caught among the emerging financial constraints, the intricacy of modern health care, and peoples' wants and worries.

In order to discuss these issues we selected a broad group of Social Work Managers whose responses to the question "What makes an Effective Social Work Administrator?" might provide answers which would be applicable to the numerous and evolving healthcare issues in urban, center-city, suburban and rural communities. The authors of these chapters have provided a stimulating and exciting group of ideas which are useful to social workers struggling with these issues in their day-to-day practice. We believe this insightful body of knowledge will act as a challenge for future social work administrators in healthcare organizations to carry on in the bold, innovative, and compassionate tradition they represent.

Crisis or Opportunity:
A Healthcare Social Work Director's
Response to Change

Neena B. Bixby, LCSW

INTRODUCTION

I am the Director of Patient Services at Huntington Memorial Hospital, a 606-bed acute care medical center serving the West San Gabriel Valley of Southern California. Patient Services deploys a broadly defined complement of social work services plus E.A.P., Child Life, Chaplaincy, Home Health, Charitable Fund programs, and Senior Care Network, a separate department. As Director, I am responsible for leading and coordinating the work of Patient Services and Senior Care Network. This article is a snapshot in time of a department on the verge of change, one whose ultimate configuration is difficult to predict but whose past accomplishments I can document with pride.

It is my hope that this synopsis of more than 20 years of experience will be of benefit both to clinicians and to scholars.

Neena B. Bixby is Director of Patient Services at Huntington Memorial Hospital, Pasadena, CA. She would like to thank W. June Simmons, Executive Vice President, Visiting Nurse Association of Los Angeles, for her invaluable assistance in refining the ideas expressed here and for her unfailing support as this article slowly took shape. Address correspondence to Neena B. Bixby, Department of Patient Services, Huntington Memorial Hospital, 100 West California Boulevard, Pasadena, CA 91109-7014.

[Haworth co-indexing entry note]: "Crisis or Opportunity: A Healthcare Social Work Director's Response to Change." Bixby, Neena B. Co-published simultaneously in *Social Work in Health Care* (The Haworth Press, Inc.) Vol. 20, No. 4, 1995, pp. 3-20; and: *Social Work Leadership in Healthcare: Directors' Perspectives* (ed: Gary Rosenberg, and Andrew Weissman), The Haworth Press, Inc., 1995, pp. 3-20. Multiple copies of this article/chapter may be purchased from The Haworth Document Delivery Center [1-800-3-HAWORTH; 9:00 a.m. - 5:00 p.m. (EST)].

This article will demonstrate that the effectiveness of a healthcare social work director is dependent upon building and maintaining the following: (1) tightly knit, dedicated management and clinical teams able to work together cooperatively and creatively; (2) a departmental culture which emphasizes innovation and the highest quality of service outcomes to patients above all else; (3) broadly-based and solid hospital and community linkages; (4) a relationship of trust and credibility with upper management and other hospital departments. These four elements make possible flexible evolution in the face of continual institutional and community challenges. They have been facilitated by continuity of personnel and philosophy from the Department's founding 22 years ago until the present and are critical to social work and managerial effectiveness.

BACKGROUND

Over the last twenty years, Southern California has undergone demographic and economic changes. These changes have fundamentally altered the healthcare social work environment. In 1975, when I started with Huntington Memorial, the majority of patients were insured or had some other means to provide reimbursement for medical services. At present, a greater percentage of patients are low income, minority, and elderly, many without medical insurance. The area's population has increased exponentially both in numbers and in degree of socioeconomic diversity. At the same time, ever more effective medical technology has made it possible to save the lives of many people who in the past would have died. These changes have been accompanied by an "astronomical rise in government controls" (Nacman, 1980). The cumulative results of these changes are a dramatic increase in demand for social work services, a deepening of the complexity of services which must be offered, and a decline in the financial resources available to deliver those services.

ENTRY INTO CURRENT POSITION

I came to Huntington Memorial Hospital in November of 1975 as the first MSW to cover the medical, surgical, and critical care areas of the hospital. Prior to that time I had been a caseworker specializing in family services at adoption and child welfare agencies in California and on the East Coast. My decision to enter medical social work was derived from a lifelong interest in healthcare whetted by exposure to medical settings through family, field placement and work in adoption and foster care.

The mid-1970's were an exciting time to enter the healthcare arena. Huntington Memorial had begun its first social work department three years before and had hired a founding director who had the opportunity to define the mission and scope of the department. In close collaboration with the director and other staff, I had the privilege to collaborate in shaping both the departmental culture and its clinical programs.

The founding Director of Patient Services was a visionary who during her tenure greatly expanded departmental responsibilities and created cutting edge, creative programming. She developed the early fiscal and administrative structure, departmental credibility, and definition of scope and purpose. Her efforts put the Department in the forefront of social work innovation. We became respected for a series of successful program design experiments.

My role during these formative years was to help develop and enhance the department's creative vision with staff support systems which emphasized a strong, positive departmental ethos as well as high standards for clinical excellence. I assumed responsibility for medical/surgical services, ER, cardiac rehab, and oncology and was also active in the development of the department's graduate social work field placement program including the field education curriculum and standards. After rising through the ranks to Assistant Director, then Associate Director, I assumed full leadership of the department in 1985.

Therefore, in the 22 years of its existence, the Department has had only two directors. Both had compatible values and goals for the department and complementary skills and strengths in realizing those goals. The founding director excelled in the creativity and marketing necessary to bring forth a new department. My talent lies in assuring excellence in departmental operation and culture. This continuity of both personnel and philosophy from creation to organizational maturation is a key component of current managerial effectiveness. It facilitated the development of a unified, positive departmental structure and operating style and was indispensable to maintenance of solid relationships with the community and other hospital departments.

DEPARTMENT OF PATIENT SERVICES MANAGEMENT STRUCTURE

Huntington Memorial Hospital is a California nonprofit healthcare institution overseen by a Board of Directors and managed by a small high level administrative team of a President, four Vice Presidents, and two Associate Administrators. During this past year, the hospital became a founding member of a new, local hospital system.

Until recently, Patient Services reported to an Associate Administrator. At present, it reports directly to the Executive Vice President. This upgrade in the reporting structure occurred when the present director assumed the additional responsibility of overseeing a second major department, the Senior Care Network.

Reporting at the senior levels has allowed the department more direct access to key decision-makers at a time when it had already gained respect and credibility within the hospital organization. This has facilitated access to a greater pool of resources as well as the ability to more easily seek administrative remedies for needed institutional changes.

The Patient Services Department is integrated into virtually all facets of hospital operation. We have achieved this level of integration through careful attention to customizing social work services to meet the particular needs of each service area of the hospital. There are two important aspects to customization: (1) rapid, dependable, round the clock responses to requests for care; and, (2) full integration of social workers into the hospital's healthcare teams and committees.

Rapid, dependable response is facilitated by broad hours of coverage (24 hour on call availability and significant on duty staffing from 8:00 a.m. to 2:00 a.m., seven days a week) and is predicated upon certain key behaviors which demonstrate respect for the other disciplines as well as for the judgment of referring departments as to the appropriate timing for social work interventions. This allows other disciplines to depend on social work for key functions because they can be certain that when help is requested, a quality response will be forthcoming within the time frame they specify.

Integration of social workers into the hospital's healthcare teams allows us to function as full-fledged professional members of the clinical system. For example, Patient Services social workers are members of the Trauma Team which is on call within a 15-minute response time 24 hours a day. In nursing units, social work staff participate in rounds and often chair patient family conferences. There are many other examples of integration which could be cited.

Extensive hospital-based committee involvement, from key leadership positions to membership participation, is an important mechanism for promoting the integration of social work into all areas of hospital functioning. Major leadership involvement has included chairing the SCAN (Suspected Child Abuse and Neglect) Team of the medical staff, leading the Oncology Community Outreach and Education Task Force, chairing the Patient Self Determination Act organizing effort to comply with the new law last year, and more short-term activities such as co-chairing, with Nursing, the re-design of the medical record for the entire institution.

Participation in hospital committees has included membership in a hospital-wide task force to re-design the methods for admission and insurance verification, participation in the design committee for inpatient case management, the Neoplastic Disease Committee of the medical staff, the Bioethics Committee, the Pediatric Professional Care Committee, and a variety of other task forces and work groups that guide the identification of appropriate changes for service areas needing revision.

CURRENT FUNCTIONS OF THE DEPARTMENT

The Patient Services Department is the one place where both staff and patients and their families can be assured that they will get help with any non-medical issue which arises during the hospital stay. Our work makes the jobs of other departments easier by addressing psychosocial obstacles to quality medical care.

The Department performs all clinical social work services for the institution, provides clinical social work and training on contract to the City of Pasadena Public Health Department and other community-based health care organizations, and conducts a variety of programs designed to provide essential psychosocial and supportive services and resources to patients which are not available through other hospital departments. These include an outpatient center for medically-related psychotherapy and biofeedback, inpatient Child Life programs, financial assistance to indigent patients, and a volunteer professional chaplaincy program. The department has primary responsibility for Discharge Planning, E.A.P., information and referral, patient advocacy, financial counseling, and clinical assessment and counseling. Patient Services is staffed by MSW's, BSW's, Discharge Planning Nurses, and Child Life Specialists. Staff see an average of 35 to 40 percent of all inpatients excluding well newborns.

MANAGEMENT STYLE AND PHILOSOPHY

The management structure is designed to develop independent judgment and accountability on the part of staff and supervisors while at the same time offering a high level of support. Every effort is made to create and sustain a respectful, collegial, warm and supportive work environment. The intention is to establish an environment that provides maximum support for, and minimum distraction from, the desire to produce good patient-centered work. The leadership system works from a coaching model. Once good staff with congruent values and clinical philosophy are selected, the group culture provides the other needed nutrients for continuing professional growth.

A major goal is to develop, and to utilize to the maximum extent, the strengths and capabilities members of the department bring to their jobs in the interest of providing the highest possible level of patient care. At the same time, we strive for team loyalty and cohesiveness since it is only through concerted team effort that the department can fulfill its responsibilities to patients and to the institution. Staff have opportunities to innovate, developing new programs and services. Opportunities for advancement by means other than management positions are offered in recognition of the multiple capabilities needed to maintain service excellence.

The administrative structure of the department consists of the Director, Assistant Director and four supervisors each of whom is responsible for a specific set of related populations. There are, for example, social work supervisors for Ambulatory Care, Rehabilitation Services (in Post Acute Care), Maternal Child Health, and Mental Health. The Assistant Director supervises Adult Medical Surgical Services.

All clinical staff are assigned to one of these managers. Each group works as a team, with each team responsible for their own particular specialty. They share resources, develop policies, manage unit relations, and collaborate clinically. Clinical staff are expected to develop strengths in a particular practice or program area so that they "own" a piece of the department and share in its leadership. Community involvement is also encouraged at this level.

The department's supervisory team has developed a vision of the mission and tasks of the department founded on deeply and mutually held values and commitments. The team meets for two hours each week during which supervisors assist one another to strategize, solve problems, and plan for the future. The emphasis at this meeting is on collaboration, shared decision-making, and mutual support. The Director meets with each of the supervisors and the Assistant Director individually for one hour per week. In addition to work with staff, supervisors are responsible for their own budgeting, are expected to sit on hospital-wide committees, and are required to be active in the community, a model congruent with that advocated by Kadushin (Kadushin, 1976).

The team-centered management structure has brought into being a shared venue for resolving challenges and creating innovative strategies to master environmental threats. The supervisory team also functions as an efficient management information gathering system. Since each supervisor is responsible for a different segment of the hospital and has relationships and access to information from a variety of perspectives, collectively they can almost always develop an "inside scoop" or useful special information that allows them to develop effective alliances as well as strategies for change on the basis of an accurate assessment of the environment.

This structure is ideally suited to fostering responsibility for and ownership of a particular specialty while at the same time ensuring accountability to higher levels of management. The nature of contemporary healthcare social work is such that swift adaptation to continual change is a precondition of professional survival. The fluid nature of the work makes rigid, centralized micro-management counterproductive. Giving staff and supervisors a high level of control over their daily tasks while at the same time requiring collaboration and accountability is an effective way to promote both excellence and flexibility (Berger, 1990).

The structure has other advantages as well. It has helped create an administrative group which is cohesive, loyal and mutually supportive and which provides consistent and complementary leadership for the entire department. As a result, the staff is unified. A strongly shared sense of purpose and loyalty to the Department by the staff is our most potent means to guarantee consistent quality care in an increasingly challenging environment.

STRATEGIES FOR THE ENHANCEMENT OF SOCIAL WORK SKILLS

Lifelong education and self-development are vital parts of staff development. All personnel are expected to develop increasingly sophisticated capabilities in their chosen specialty. In addition, they must acquire a broadly-based understanding of how the hospital and the Department of Patient Services work. Although the Department routinely provides internal continuing education, staff are expected to seek out additional outside learning opportunities.

Enhancement of the skills which new staff bring to the job begins with orientation. Our department prides itself on a supportive, comprehensive and orderly orientation process. New staff have the opportunity to orient to the department for 6 to 10 days before picking up cases. This allows for a thoughtful and comprehensive introduction to the hospital, office, to staff and the culture, and to programs within the Department as well as special programs reporting to the department such as Patient Assistance, Senior Care Network, and Huntington Hospital Home Care. An opportunity to learn the history of the department and its philosophy is provided as well as a time to become familiar with the area to which the social worker will be assigned.

For example, when a new clinician joins the Neonatal Social Work Team, the group assigned to work with the families of newborn infants, it is important to become familiar not only with the Neonatal Social Work Team but also with the Maternal Child Health Team of which Neonatal is a part. Staff then must orient to the Neonatal Unit of Huntington Memorial and must become thoroughly acquainted with the Pasadena Health Department's Prenatal Clinic, because a number of patients will transfer to the hospital from there; Pediatrics, because some of the neonates will go on to Pediatrics; and High Risk Infant Follow-up, where a number of the Neonatal patients will be seen following discharge. In addition, there are referrals to the Outpatient Peds Rehab Area and so the new staff member must become familiar with this area also.

The Neonatal social worker must understand the work of colleagues in Child Life in order to make this program available to the siblings of neonates when they go in to meet their brothers and sisters for the first time. Knowledge of the work of the SCAN Team is necessary in addition. The worker becomes acquainted with the office staff, the statistical program, policies and procedures, and simple logistics such as how to find the way between the office and the Neonatal Unit which is a block away.

All staff are supervised individually on a once a week basis for at least a year or until they are licensed, whichever comes first. After that, they have an individualized schedule. They also participate twice a month in their social work team meeting. These important team meetings include a pooling of information about activities within the clinical area of focus, sharing of new resources, collaboration and discussion of difficult cases and other matters. In addition, the meeting is an opportunity for the social work supervisor to share with the team trends across the whole hospital and issues from the social work management team. These matters may be discussed in the entire department staff meeting, but I consider it important to also discuss them in the smaller team. Here, there is an opportunity for candid asking of questions and in-depth exploration of clinician concerns and issues.

Each member of the clinical staff is assigned to one of three inter-team and interdisciplinary groups of department staff, each headed by a clinical specialist, which meet monthly to provide training to staff on clinical issues. These monthly clinical specialist seminars focus on discussion of clinical material. The format might vary from case presentation to review of journal articles to an in-depth discussion on a particular clinical issue brought up by a member of the group.

Staff are encouraged to contribute to their own clinical learning through attending outside seminars or other professional development opportunities. Supervisors and staff regularly assess learning needs. If these needs cannot be accommodated in-house, then a mutually satisfactory arrangement can be negotiated which may include leave time or assistance in obtaining the necessary educational funding. The primary concern is that staff have the ongoing opportunity to upgrade their skills to the extent that this is compatible with effective patient services.

Opportunities for program development are a long-standing Patient Services tradition. Staff are encouraged regularly to identify change initiatives that emerge in the course of clinical work. For instance, a staff member identified the need for bereavement services and helped the hospital establish a bereavement group for families. In another instance, a staff member was concerned that there were no appropriate resources to help children of terminally ill parents to cope. In response, a new program, *I Count Too,* was initiated. *New Directions,* our outpatient medically-related biofeedback and psychotherapy program, was developed and is currently operated by social work staff to provide these services for the community.

Such opportunities allow staff to test new skills and to maintain their professional integrity through assuring a complete array of services for populations that inspire their concerns. These are closely mentored and monitored activities which provide coaching opportunities from a variety of experts in the community or the department. Every effort is made to facilitate these role diversification, growth and innovation experiences.

These efforts are important not only for skills development but as a means to maintain a high level of staff morale. Such activities strengthen staff's sense of empowerment in the face of shrinking resources and build a sense of ownership and pride in departmental programs which have been successfully implemented. These are then transformed into new services which tend to yield a high sense of satisfaction for the team as well as the innovator.

EDUCATION OF SOCIAL WORK STUDENTS

Since 1975, the Department of Patient Services has been a training site for Masters level social work students. Currently, students are placed from the three schools of social work in Los Angeles County: the University of California, Los Angeles (UCLA); the University of Southern California (USC); and California State University, Long Beach (CSULB). The department takes from one to four students at a time. Each is expected to complete three rotations, one of which is always an evening a week in the Emergency Department. Each student has a field instructor and may also have preceptors in particular areas depending on their chosen rotation. The students must meet with their field instructor a minimum of once a week on a regularly assigned time basis and with the preceptors in their area for additional time as needed. Students attend a weekly student seminar developed by a variety of members of the department's clinical staff. The seminar format alternates, between a discussion group where students bring in clinical questions and case material for discussion, and a lecture on a specific issue by a staff member.

In addition to the student placements, Patient Services staff have varying degrees of involvement with the local Schools of Social Work. Currently, three members of the staff teach at the schools. Six devote time to committees at the schools in an attempt to influence both the direction of the curriculum and the concentrations.

Staff are eager to collaborate with the schools. Collaboration offers a unique chance to shape the nature and quality of the educational experience of students. As professional social workers, staff feel a solid commitment to the education of the students who will succeed them. They experience a very strong motivation to assure the availability of a qualified work force for openings that will come up in the future. It is also an opportunity to form relationships with students and, in doing so, to establish a very positive reputation for the department within the profession. These forms of staff involvement with social work students improve the likelihood of the department being viewed as an attractive source of employment and thus place the department in a position to draw in talented new graduate social workers.

In addition to direct student instruction and involvement in schools of social work, the supervisors in the department are very active in the Southern California Chapter of the Society for Social Work Administrators in Health Care, the only administrative group available for healthcare social work managers. Their involvement offers exposure to other administrators which develops their thinking through giving them an opportunity to share issues and solutions to problems with other leaders. It provides them with a broad overview of major healthcare issues, the effects of these issues on social work, as well as the critical initiatives undertaken in the field to respond to these environmental factors.

THE PLANNING PROCESS

The Department's basic planning mechanism is the weekly two-hour management team meeting during which all planning issues are raised. The process is informed by staff input received in the course of regular individual supervision and the group team meetings. Additional issues might surface in other contexts such as the clinical specialist meetings or the broader staff meetings of the department.

A highly structured agenda has been developed for this team meeting. The agenda encourages depth of discussion as well as continuity of content and activities from week to week. Individual supervisors take responsibility for leading components of departmental activity and development efforts and bring reports and materials to the meeting for discussion in their areas of responsibility.

For example, one supervisor is responsible for the departmental quality improvement program. This individual brings quality improvement materials to the meeting and reviews them with the team. The team offers input into quality improvement materials design, analysis and needed changes that quality activities identify. Another example is the development of the management information system. This initiative was led by one supervisor. It received input from the entire department and the collaboration of the full social work management team over a period of a year.

As issues and needs are identified, they are brought to the attention of other department leaders and/or senior hospital management whose input is sought. In addition, the supervisors and the department head often will engage in shared thinking and planning with leaders in the various specialty areas in which they work and will obtain advice from medical staff in the course of their work.

The budgeting process is an extensive one which occurs primarily, at the planning level, through the social work management team. It takes several months to complete. The process consists of environmental assessment to identify opportunities and threats occurring throughout the hospital as they affect social work services. It is also informed by the general identification of needed changes and reallocation of existing resources within the department and across programs as needs in the environment change in the course of the year.

This overall structure rests on the strong foundation created annually during a one-day strategic planning retreat for the social work management team. In this session, which is self-led, the participants discuss the major issues and challenges facing the department and the hospital. They refine these issues and try to prioritize key areas needing action. Action plans are then developed by the team and the work is distributed among management team members. Finally, the resulting structure is implemented through the normal channels and reviewed during the weekly management team meetings.

KEY COMPONENTS OF THE COLLABORATIVE NETWORK

As noted, a great deal of collaboration occurs through the involvement of leaders of other areas of the hospital. The department collaborates with key nursing leaders, department heads and a variety of other segments of senior management. The supervisors also maintain networks in the ranks of direct service staff both within and outside of social work. These supervisors enjoy very intensive close collaborative relationships with the administrators and clinical leaders within the programs their staff serve. For example, the Rehabilitation social work supervisor is a member of the multi-disciplinary team that operates within the Rehabilitation and Skilled Nursing divisions of the hospital. There, the supervisor participates as a collaborator to obtain counsel and input from others and to offer social work influence in the planning and decision-making in these other programs. The same situation pertains in Maternal Child Health and other specialty areas of the hospital.

COMMUNITY LINKAGES

The Department developed and maintains very strong community ties. These ties are essential to good service provision. Community involvement, a requirement for all professional social work staff, allows social workers to develop additional facets of professional expertise. It enhances the financial viability and range of services of the department through bringing in outside contracts. Most importantly, it enables us to offer better service to patients by smoothing the transition from the hospital setting to community and home. Good reciprocal relationships anchor the effort to advocate for patients and their special needs.

Professional social work staff are expected to be involved in at least one community agency. They are given wide latitude in choice of the involvement – anything from sitting on the board of a local agency to participating in a committee or consortium. The idea of networking is stressed so that the department may build enduring relationships in the community and strong linkages to integrate systems of care.

We have sought to develop contracts outside the hospital to provide social work services in the community. We did this originally by providing services to our local Visiting Nurse Association and to a small community hospital. In recent years, we have developed contracts to provide social work staffing for the Pasadena Health Department Prenatal Clinics and as consultants in the state Comprehensive Perinatal Services Program. We recently completed a social work services contract as part of the community coalition that received Ryan White funding for an early intervention HIV Clinic.

The growing complexity of problems in the community has required development of close working relationships among individuals and institutions charged with seemingly unrelated tasks. For example, mentally ill, violent homeless patients are sometimes brought to Huntington Memorial's Emergency Room. Neither the hospital nor our department is equipped to provide for such patients. They must be sent to County USC Medical Center where the appropriate staff and facilities are available. In order to get them there, we have had to develop closer working relationships with the Pasadena Police Department and Paramedics for transportation to the County facility.

Our community linkages are a significant factor which enables us to offer quality services even as the financial resources supporting such services continue to diminish. Because we provide unremunerated help and support to organizations such as Hospice of Pasadena, Visiting Nurse Association of Los Angeles, and the American Red Cross, Pasadena Chapter, these organizations in turn help our patients.

Hospice of Pasadena turned to Patient Services for help with their strategic planning. This collaboration helped identify some special unmet needs of patient groups. As a result, Hospice was willing to redefine its focus from sole concentration on the terminally ill to also serving the seriously ill. This enabled Hospice to begin providing special volunteer support to patients in the medical center, patients utilizing outpatient services, and patients recently discharged from the hospital to home. This change of both emphasis and practice on the part of Hospice created a new referral resource for our social workers and for the other Patient Services staff while at the same time strengthening the Hospice program.

Because of the ongoing mutual support built into the department's relationship with other agencies, a formal linkage may evolve in direct response to a clinician's immediate need for a key resource for a patient. For example, the Senior Care Network, which reports to the Director of Patient Services, was looking for a way to follow-up on certain hospital patients after they had returned home. Senior Care Network and Patient Services were able to develop a cross-employment relationship so that in-home follow-up by hospital staff could be provided through the hospital's Home Health arrangement with Visiting Nurse Association.

RESEARCH

Due to the extreme pressure experienced in the clinical setting in this age of shrinking resources, the department has focused its efforts on maintaining and developing excellence in clinical service delivery. The data collection and staffing resources necessary to conduct research are simply not available due to funding constraints. Therefore, most scientific inquiry done in the Department is initiated through linkages with academic institutions. Collaborative studies in cancer and pain management have been carried out with USC and UCLA through our outpatient medically-related psychotherapy and biofeedback programs. The department's role in these investigations has been to facilitate academic researcher access to clinical subjects within outpatient settings. In addition, we have been willing to test special service models, such as a new format for assisting patients with pain management.

SKILLS AND KNOWLEDGE NECESSARY FOR SUCCESS

Some key skills emanate from the social work director's views on the following: the nature of social workers' role within healthcare settings; the leadership responsibilities of the social work director within both the institution and the department; and the most effective instrumental means to realize optimal social worker and leadership roles.

In my view, the mission of social work within healthcare settings is to contribute to high quality patient outcomes. The way to accomplish this is twofold: maintain a strong, unambiguous sense of professional integrity and mission; and, make social work assistance available throughout the hospital in such a way that services are customized to the needs of patients, family members of patients, and hospital staff.

From this point of view, the most critical social work director skill is the ability to sustain a departmental culture that values high quality patient care above all else. Sustaining this culture requires the ability to maintain the morale and energy among the staff needed to support intensive patient advocacy and quality outcomes; and, to maintain supportive structures within the department which en-

courage professional growth and which allow individuals to identify and work through personal and professional issues in a construc-
tive manner such that overall team morale is not compromised and
to do this in a time when fiscal resources are shrinking.

Other skills are exercised outside the department, in the context
of a hospital environment which has become increasingly conflictu-
al and competitive. In this environment, it is essential to have a clear
sense of professional integrity and departmental mission and to
maintain a long-term view in which setbacks are seen not as fail-
ures, but as necessary steps toward the eventual achievement of
goals consistent with professional integrity and mission. The social
work director should have the capacity to respect, work with, and
draw on the diverse strengths of the various departments within the
institution. Doing so requires picking one's battles and standing
one's ground in the face of conflict while preserving vital, long-
term relationships throughout the institution. It requires the capacity
to remain calm in the face of adversity or the unknown; strong
negotiating skills; identification and management of issues requiring advocacy or change initiatives; and establishment of administrative credibility through fiscal knowledgeability and personal responsibility and demonstration of top quality clinical outcomes in
the face of shrinking resources.

These skills are not easily cultivated. They evolve from an in-
depth understanding of the social workers, the hospital, and the
needs of patients, derived from years of experience in medical
social work. I consider myself very fortunate to have had the opportunity to have been a member of the line staff at Huntington Hospital as well as having the role of supervising a number of staff in the
institution as I moved up the administrative ladder to my current
position. I feel strongly that there is no substitute for having walked
in the shoes of the staff for whom one is responsible.

In addition, having been a staff member in this institution for
many, many years has provided me the opportunity to have a
number of professional and personal relationships with other hospital employees that stand me in good stead when negotiating and
working on interdepartmental committees and task forces. These
linkages, so critical to our departmental functioning, can only be

developed slowly as trust and modes of cooperation mature over time.

Above all, there can be no substitute for love of the work. Any effectiveness I can claim as a social work director flows from my great enjoyment of the profession. There's nothing else like it.

REFERENCES

Berger, Candyce S. "Enhancing Social Work Influence in the Hospital: Identifying Sources of Power." *Social Work in Health Care*, Vol. 15, No. 2, 1990.

Jansson, Bruce S., and Simmons, June. "Building Departmental or Unit Power Within Human Service Organizations: Empirical Findings and Theory Building." *Administration in Social Work*, Vol. 8, No. 3, 1984.

Kadushin, Alfred. *Supervision in Social Work*. New York: Columbia University Press, 1976.

Nacman, Martin. "Reflections of a Social Work Administrator on the Opportunities of Crisis." *Social Work in Health Care*, Vol. 6, No. 1, 1980.

Wax, John. "Clinical Contributions to Administrative Practice." In *Advancing Social Work Practice in the Health Care Field. Emerging Issues and New Perspectives*, Gary Rosenberg and Helen Rehr, eds. New York: The Haworth Press, Inc. 1983.

Reflections on Effective Leadership:
Strains and Successes, Strategies and Styles

Susan Blumenfield, DSW

The advertisement for a current business success book, *Leadership Secrets of Attila the Hun* (Roberts, 1993), states: "Attila's advice to IBM: Winning tribes are led by chieftains who understand that no tribe is lucky enough to meet only less well-led opponents." This concise message captures the themes of many current leadership articles with references to military geniuses who are both brilliant strategists and are lucky. Such metaphors are difficult to incorporate into an article about social work leadership in health care because social work is characterized as a helping and caring profession with a compassionate image, and a dedication to humanistic society. Yet, we all know that a number of fine, competent social work leaders have not survived in today's health care world, or have, at least, decided to resign. Leadership in today's health care social work may require the energy and strategic skills of an Attila, but it must be tempered with the vision of Jane Adams, the intellect of Gordon Hamilton, the know-how of a Harvard MBA, with a dash of Joan of Arc fortitude and early Napoleonic luck. Is such a fusion of aptitudes possible?

The assignment at hand calls for a personal reflection on my own

Susan Blumenfield is Director, Department of Social Work Services and Associate Director of Clinical Operations, The Mount Sinai Hospital, and is Associate Professor of Community Medicine at The Mount Sinai Medical School.

[Haworth co-indexing entry note]: "Reflections on Effective Leadership: Strains and Successes, Strategies and Styles." Blumenfield, Susan. Co-published simultaneously in *Social Work in Health Care* (The Haworth Press, Inc.) Vol. 20, No. 4, 1995, pp. 21-37; and: *Social Work Leadership in Healthcare: Directors' Perspectives* (ed: Gary Rosenberg, and Andrew Weissman), The Haworth Press, Inc., 1995, pp. 21-37. Multiple copies of this article/chapter may be purchased from The Haworth Document Delivery Center [1-800-3-HAWORTH; 9:00 a.m. - 5:00 p.m. (EST)].

21

leadership styles, skills, and philosophy, all of which exist in a specific administrative background, the Mount Sinai Medical Center in New York City. It is written in a time of heightened national attention to health care, as consumers and health care providers alike await crucial governmental policy decisions on access and service delivery issues. This tension pushes the climate of a constantly frenzied environment to an almost insupportable crisis limit. As unnerving as the situation is, however, it does provide a unique opportunity to take a close-range look at my own repertoire of leadership principles and skills as I try to sort out information, to decide on strategies, to balance options with long range vision and immediate survival, all against a background of uncertainty. Some degree of uncertainty and flux is expectable in the leadership experience, but the changes that loom large in health care signal, like the drum rolls before battle in Henry V, that a full scale test of leadership is at hand.

This narrative of leadership cannot, however, be a leap into the dramatic present. Oliver Wendell Holmes said "When I want to understand what is happening today or try to decide what will happen tomorrow, I look back." Looking back on the pertinent historical aspects of departmental and personal professional development becomes a major expenditure of attention. In this discussion, an expenditure that is vital in comprehending, coping, and mastering the current demands on social work leadership in health care.

BACKGROUND: THE HOSPITAL AND THE DEPARTMENT OF SOCIAL WORK SERVICES

The Mount Sinai Medical Center is a major academic institution that exists with the inherent strain of being a first-rate academic medical center providing tertiary care, excellence in teaching and research, and, as well, being a hospital in a community needing primary care and prevention services. The Director of the Department of Social Work Services has the responsibility to design, implement, and maintain a comprehensive program that is in keeping with the mission of the institution, and at the same time meets the needs of the populations served.

Today there are approximately 175 social workers in the Department of Social Work Services, and a support staff of about 25. The Department of Social Work Services is well integrated into both the Mount Sinai Hospital and the Mount Sinai School of Medicine. There are many reasons for this, probably the most important being the innovative leadership of my predecessors and the original mission of the hospital when it was founded in 1852 and the medical school when it came into being in 1968. In addition to social service support for hospital inpatient, outpatient and community programs, social workers provide a broad array of functions within the institution such as, employee assistance counseling, wellness programs, community outreach efforts, health education, and organizational development functions. In the hospital, social work services and perspectives become integrated in institutional decision making on scope, direction, and planning of services. It means that I, like some of my predecessors hold a hospital administrative title as well as that of Director of the Department of Social Work Services. In addition to being the Director of the Department of Social Work Services I am also an Associate Director of the hospital with other departments–Patient Representatives, the Rape Crisis Intervention Program, and Psychiatric Rehabilitation–reporting to me. I hold an Associate Professor rank within the faculty of the Division of Social Work in the Department of Community Medicine. Approximately thirty social workers from the staff are also members of this faculty, again allowing social work some say in the affairs of the medical school. Finally, I serve as a consultant to the Auxiliary Board, an organization that oversees significant service and educational functions at the medical center, and which has been a strong ally to the department of social work services at Mount Sinai from its inception in the early part of the twentieth century.

Much of the foundation of our department lies in the vision, energies, and flexibility of social work administrators, past and present. Chief among these are Doris Siegel who came in 1953 as the first professional social work director. Through her leadership social work achieved a professional status that was integrated into patient care and hospital policy decisions. Helen Rehr, D.S.W. continued that leadership, as the era of professional accountability appeared, introducing key practice concepts for high risk screening and peer review mechanisms, along with initiating programs for consumer advocacy, research, and evaluation. Gary Rosenberg, Ph.D. was next in line of succession leading the department with managerial excellence, blending quality, self-directed practice with financial and marketing skills in the first stages of cost containment and DRG's, and expanding the application of social work knowledge and skill to the highest levels in hospital management. Rosenberg (1987) describes his leadership insight thus, "The successful social work departments have been those which have understood how to mesh the goals of department advocacy and the goals of the medical center. . . . One can identify oneself with the point of view of the department, and with the point of view of the patient it serves, particularly the disadvantaged or those in need of care, but always within a framework of understanding the conflicting needs of the organization as well as the organization's priorities and value system" (p. 80-81). Andrew Weissman, D.S.W. followed and with Gary Rosenberg brought marketing skills into the forefront of social work management (Rosenberg and Weissman, 1984).

TRANSITION TO LEADERSHIP

In 1978 I came to the Department of Social Work Services as a part-time consultant with a specialty in Geriatrics. The charge to the new geriatric team—a geriatrician, geriatric nurse clinician, and myself—was to develop educational programs in geriatrics for social workers and other health professionals. We established electives for medical students, a summer stipend educational experience for medical and social work students, and weekly teaching rounds for all disciplines on both a medical and a psychiatry unit. I initiated a Gerontological Journal Club for social workers which became part of the continuing educational fabric of the department and continues to this day. Thus, in my first years at Mount Sinai I saw myself chiefly as a clinician who was embarking on a clinical/educational project.

Although as part of my doctoral dissertation I had set up a hospital program involving volunteers and in my initial educational role at Mount Sinai there was a great deal of program planning, I certainly did not see myself as an "administrator." In fact, I had practically no formal courses or real experience in administration up to this point. Informally, my managerial skills had been honed early on as a camp counselor, and later in raising a family of three children. Balancing family responsibilities with work demands also took organizational skills. In those personal experiences I had acquired a solid respect for skills in balancing individual and group needs, for recognizing developmental differences and demands for "fairness," and for making my own demands as explicit and reasonable as possible. These may have been "volunteer leadership" encounters, but they were helpful in providing a sound basis for subsequent professional administration.

In 1983, the grant through which I had been funded was coming to an end. I was on the Medical School Faculty but how further stay at Mount Sinai could be supported was in question. The position as Assistant Director for Medical/Surgical social work became available and it was offered to me. For a person who had never seen herself as an "administrator," I decided to take the risk and to accept this new and somewhat alien challenge. The position in Med/Surg carried with it responsibilities as Discharge Planning Coordinator for the medical center as well. I remember so clearly the trepidation I felt in the first few days of this new role, but I remember even more vividly my own shock about two weeks later when I found I was actually thrilled and excited in my multiple pursuits within the department, with supervisors and line staff, and within the larger hospital sphere as I dealt with nursing and medical directors, quality assurance personnel, and hospital administrators. I had never before experienced such full use of my professional self. Suddenly I was in a position to provide leadership to a large part of the department, to come up with new ideas and influence their being carried out, to create educational packages to meet needs of workers as I perceived them, and to create a new climate in the program area. It was a surprisingly heady experience.

In retrospect, responsibility for this program area and discharge planning provided a paradigm for the director role I was later to assume. In those roles, I began to learn the significance of balancing, balancing the demands of the staff for professional integrity with the demands of the hospital and regulatory forces for cost containment and length of stay controls, balancing fiscal realities with needs for resources and rewards for performance excellence, balancing my clinical sensitivity to patient and family concerns with institutional limitations and priorities. In 1986 I became a Senior Associate Director in the department. Throughout these stages I was most fortunate to have Drs. Rosenberg, Rehr, and Weissman, as my mentors and models, and the fact that they are still available for guidance and discussion is infinitely helpful. They are all, fortunately, guardian angels with a strong flair for risk and creativity. On the other hand however, their very strong personalities and achievements presented a challenge as I attempted to crystallize my own identity as a leader and provide an imprint within the department.

THE BEGINNING PHASE OF LEADERSHIP

In discussing executive entry, Austin (1989) emphasizes the process of learning about self in the process of providing leadership. He notes also that the entry process is closely linked to the way in which "executives help to create a vision and to position an organization for the future" with special attention to building trust with people in and out of the organization (p. 56). As I began my director role I was conscious of my "clinical" proclivities, especially the priority I put on the catalytic, or behind the scenes force for change. I recognized consciously that leadership called not only for visibility but promotional visibility. I also recognized that I would have to learn new skills in finance and the fiscal components of administration. I did have a beginning awareness in this area, but up to this time I had relied on others for the ultimate knowledge. In order to learn more, I found that asking others about their work, styles and philosophies was helpful. I read a great deal about leadership, organizations and management styles. I even went through some work books on budgeting and convinced the institution to send me to the University of Pennsylvania's Wharton School of Business for a week long course on finance for the non-financial manager. All of this was helpful in providing orientation to parts of my new role and to familiarizing me with a new vocabulary. The new concepts were, of course, built on my already existing individual personality structure and the values, skills and knowledge of the social work profession. I felt as though the professional process, of collecting information, formulating an assessment, and creating an intervention to help to solve a problem, influence change, or create new responses, was extremely applicable to the broader organization. It was important too, early on, to create a vision for departmental functioning that would preserve the rich traditions and strengths of the past while adding new strengths, increased depth and a new tone which could carry us into the future. Continuing the rich legacy of the department would be a challenge; finding a new vision toward which to aspire was even more daunting.

One of my early additions was the creation of a departmental breakfast. It was an enlargement of a Med/Surg tradition that I had instituted and that had proven to be conducive to joy and good fellowship. In a department the size of ours, there are few opportunities to get everyone together just to meet, greet, and bask in the excitement of our shared enterprise. No grand rounds, no long speeches, only the stipulation that each member of the department meet and get to know at least two people they hadn't known before, as well as socializing with those they knew. As I drove to the first departmental breakfast, struggling to think of a catchy welcome message, I experienced a kind of Joan of Arc "hearing of voices." The "voice" was an advertisement on the radio for the *Wall Street Journal,* a voice that proclaimed that the readers of that newspaper were "faster, tougher and smarter." It was suddenly clear that social work in health care had become "faster," "tougher" and "smarter," but that was not enough. The message I ultimately delivered was based on that concept. We had become faster. We were more efficient. We valued cost-effectiveness and we used technology to speed our work. Yet, we could not run so fast that we never stopped to reflect, to see where we had come from and to be sure where we were going. We had become tougher. We did not wear our hearts on our sleeves. We could converse in the language of business and finance. We even read the *Wall Street Journal.* But, we could not be so tough that we were immune to others' pain, or accepted the unacceptable. We could not be so tough that we stood alone. We needed to stand together, to be there for each other and to work collectively. We had become smarter. We held more roles and spoke more languages. We had developed new strategies to meet new needs. We had attended courses, institutes and doctoral programs. But, if we lost our passion we would have lost it all. We would become automatons, not social workers. We would do less good than we were capable of. Thus, the early direction I tried to set was that we needed to be faster and reflective, tougher and collective, smarter and passionate. It was just the right note for the breakfast, and over time the message has stayed with me, creating an image that is truly my departmental ideal, or at least preliminary vision.

An early leadership task was to evaluate departmental structure, and in doing so I found that two key units were without assistant directors. This fact led me to a decision to go outside the department to fill these vacancies. This decision seemed to be strongly opposed to the building trust principle, in that hiring from inside for managerial positions had become an unwritten law, thus far, in the department. However, it was important to hire the best people possible for these jobs. I felt the need to get "fastest, toughest and smartest" candidates with clinical, administrative and research strengths who could help advance the vision. This need overrode the cozier principle. It also became a first taste of "owning responsibility" for unpopular decisions. It was important to reinforce the principle of elevating competence at the same time that equity in opportunity, open participation in planning, and emphasis on the quality of services provided were addressed. It was also essential that the people with whom I would be working most closely would be professionals who could infuse continued high regard for the quality of service to people, the need for research and reflection on what we do, and concern for staff, the ultimate providers of our product. In other words, it was clear that senior managers would need to own the vision and help to shape it.

From my earliest days as director, I tried to cultivate a senior management group that would not only be strong separately and exceedingly competent in running their specific program areas, but also would together become a "think tank" of participants with total departmental interests at heart. It is inherently difficult for people to hold both the partisan and the collective views simultaneously, but it was an important goal and has provided a richness and strength which would not have been possible otherwise. Over the years we have grappled as a group with budget cuts and their implementation, with reactions to staff concerns, common patient problems, locational moves, need for policy changes and clarification, the support of research endeavors, educating ourselves about future trends and even creating innovations such as a "clinical career ladder" to recognize and reward clinical social work as it occurs in an academically oriented setting. The give and take is extraordinary and richness of thinking always ultimately produces outcomes of higher quality than any one person could accomplish alone. The participatory style is one I have favored from the beginning and continue to favor and value. However, as the collective reflection leads to recommendations, I still feel ultimately responsible for each decision. Certainly, all are clear that it is with me that the "buck stops." But prior to that moment, the thinking, debating and planning are valued in producing a better "buck" and ideas more possible of real implementation.

When I review this entry phase I find myself comforted by an article I read in the *Harvard Business Review* by William Peace (1991) with the apt title "The Hard Work of Being a Soft Manager." The author is reassuring as he says "self confidence can be a cover for arrogance or fear, resolute can be a code word for autocratic and hard-nosed can be thick-skinned" (p. 40). While emphasizing the importance of the qualities of intelligence, energy, confidence, and responsibility, Peace also stresses "being vulnerable to the give and take of ordinary emotional crossfire and intellectual disagreement makes us more human, more credible, and more open to change" (p. 47).

TAKING HOLD AND MOVING ON

As I took hold of departmental leadership, marketing theory became a new and exciting conceptual framework which helped me to bridge the fluctuations of institutional demands and professional survival. This construct made the visibility and promotional aspects of leadership not only palatable but exciting. Seeing clinical practice as a product of value made me enthusiastic, not defensive about the services that I truly felt were needed by special populations and groups. This reframing of social work values and services has become firmly integrated into my leadership persona.

My management style and philosophy have continued. However, I have become clearer about what areas are givens and have little room for discussion, and what areas need real work. Often subsets of the management group will do initial thinking which can be brought back to the whole. On many issues, committees are created which consist of staff members, preceptors and senior managers to work on new ideas and make recommendations.

The structure of the department, with slight alterations, continues as it has in the past. There are five program areas, each headed by an assistant director: Med/Surg, Ambulatory Care, Maternal and Child Health, Psychiatry, and Adolescent Health. These correspond roughly to the administrative groupings in the hospital. Under each of the Assistant Directors are several units, led by Preceptors, which are comprised of eight to fourteen workers. Another area led by an Assistant Director is our Information Systems which has grown in both equipment and function in the last few years. There is an Associate Director responsible for Administrative Operations including Information Systems, support staff, budget, etc., and a Director of Education & Quality Assurance who heads up these enterprises. I meet weekly with the Senior Management Group which allows communication about what is going on as well as working sessions to create policy and direction. I also meet monthly with the Preceptors to provide me with a direct link to this most important middle-management group. Thus communications are both up and down within the hierarchical structure of this large department as well as across via committees, task forces and groups on which all levels of staff are represented.

One of the new communications devices I initiated soon after becoming Director was an annual "State of The Department" message. It seemed important that all staff should hear directly from me at one of our monthly Grand Rounds. I wanted staff to hear directly from me about what had been going on in the past year, what our accomplishments had been and the directions in which we would be heading. This was done to communicate, to provide recognition of achievements and to inspire to further efforts and new directions. By 1990, I felt it was important to articulate specific goals toward which people could work and against which accomplishments could be measured.

Thus in the annual departmental address in September, 1990 I enunciated explicit departmental goals :

- to enhance the provision of excellent clinical services;
- to develop an organizational environment which fosters creativity and initiative;
- to develop strategies for recruitment and retention;
- to develop an information system strategy which enhances decision making and increases research productivity; and
- to increase revenue production.

With these goals I also introduced a plan to use focus groups with the staff over the next year, so that the staff could be more directly involved in goal realization. It was also important to break into the usual hierarchical communication patterns for richer interchange. The focus group methodology provided important information on our strengths and assets. It also allowed for staff at all levels to interact and create recommendations for improvement in many areas. The suggestions brought forth have provided basic guidelines for further discussion, work, and change in the department. Having explicit goals, having staff participation in the planning to reach them and in the implementation of these new ideas has allowed change to occur.

Goal measurement is crucial, a compass for steering that keeps us on course, not prey to veering off course on minor winds that distract and distort. In this way we continue to look at what we are doing in relation to our goals and try to modify as necessary as we concentrate on the work environment, the research development, the practice enhancements, etc.

GOALS AND ACCOMPLISHMENTS

The Department of Social Work Services has been noted for excellence in patient care, education, administration, and research for many decades. My purpose at this writing is not to delineate the department in its complete scope, but rather to list programmatic innovations over the past five years, as well as the strengthening of programs that were already in place when I came to the department.

This is in keeping with the ideas of Hinterhuber and Popp (1992) who point out "sooner or later, all great business accomplishments are surpassed" (p. 111). But new directives, initiatives, questions raised and staff selected, provide the more permanent legacy for management and leadership.

In growth and development over the past few years the Department of Social Work Services has paralleled the Mount Sinai Medical Center itself, constantly adding new staff and new programs that keep faith with both hospital and departmental missions for excellence in patient care, education, and research. We have maintained a population perspective in both tertiary and primary care, demonstrating that social workers can be efficient deliverers of quality service and at the same time can be innovative practitioners in community outreach and health education programs. Our staff has confronted all the social dragons of current society, Aids, drugs, limited access to health care, restrictions on length of stay and home services, with vigor and dedication, sometimes as part of medical teams and sometimes as solo players. A crucial component of leadership, both from myself and senior management, has been to support and reward these efforts, maintaining a positive up-beat spirit at a time when it would be easy to succumb to a mood of pessimism. We all hear the Cassandra voices of doom which constantly hover over social work departments.

Two areas of note marking new directions within our department are the enhancement of the work environment and the infusion of research thinking in a larger group of staff. For example, workers asked for more effective communication. We created a quarterly newsletter through which a staff editorial board reports in depth about clinical or program innovations, research endeavors, and policy dilemmas. We added a monthly calendar of events listing courses, journal clubs, group discussions, and special projects which will occur in the following month. Formal courses, grand rounds, journal clubs and open preceptor learning experiences have been supplemented by clinical consultation series, special lunch hour policy lectures and one shot topical sessions as issues arise like concerns about T.B. or parameters of managed care. Committees which are made up of staff from all areas meet regularly and report back to their units. These include the Staff Rep, Social policy, Peer

Review and Educational Planning Committees. Task forces have been created to deal with specific issues like enhancing our orientation program for new workers or working on innovative ideas for worker coverage.

Linking research to practice has been another goal on which we have worked. In order to advance the quality of practice I felt it was important to help workers see how their every day practice was based on their own reflection on practice. We discuss this during the hiring process and continually throughout the workers tenure in the department. We have also tried to provide structures to assist in raising questions and in looking for answers in an analytic, objective manner. Courses in doing research have been established for workers. Others were set up for preceptors in order to help them pursue their own questions and help to stimulate workers in looking at their practice. Creating a Senior Management Research Advisory Group and supporting the continued services of a research consultant have produced a "can-do" atmosphere for all staff who wish to pursue research activities. Consultation and continuing education courses in research have strengthened this direction, as well as offering the back-up services of a sophisticated information service. The result is that at this time research has become an expectable practice component for all staff. This ties in other expectations for excellence that we have begun to enunciate to staff via a career ladder format.

After many years of work and many frustrating attempts, the knowledge gained from these and the other changes taking place has enabled us to develop a viable Clinical Career Ladder. Prior to this, workers had been able to receive recognition and monetary reward by moving into management positions or even becoming faculty members, but defining and recognizing advancing clinical practice had always eluded our grasp. Suddenly an epiphany occurred. We realized that advancing clinical practice in an academic setting had to take in the breadth and depth of what is really expected. Not only does expertise in working with patients, families and collaborative staff increase, but ways of viewing situations, ability to teach, question, and come to answers, advance as well. We have just defined different stages of advancing practice by establishing criteria for each. We have also been able to obtain hospital administrative agreement to reward monetarily workers who meet the criteria and reach new levels of practice. While we are just at the beginning stages of implementation of the new Clinical Career Ladder, such a prospect is most challenging for management and most rewarding for staff.

INTO THE BREACH OF THE HERE AND NOW

The above summation and review provides a momentary sense of satisfaction and well-being, but, as I have pointed out in the introduction, the overriding climate of crisis and profound change in health care is pervasive and the implications for social work remain nebulous. Russell Baker, *The New York Times* columnist, captures the prevailing mood in health care best, as he comments "Listening to experts on the health care problem is like reading computer manuals. Their brilliance is obvious and indisputable, and I for one–I won't speak for you–can't understand a thing they say." In the environment of a large academic medical center, however, even humor cannot dispel the anxiety that permeates. The usual managerial alliances are muted, and for a time directors and high level managers are quietly attentive and reflective. In this time of review and reflection I am conscious of the following leadership concepts; style, use of information and affect, power, strategy, and vision. Let me expand on each of these concepts.

As I engage my Senior Management Team in serious brainstorming we review the social work product in its strengths and weaknesses. In discharge planning and community outreach, in counseling and advocacy we score high. The area of funding and revenue production is the vital question in new insurance models, especially in out-patient services. With all the questions and guesses, we must assemble a list of strategies that convey creativity and flexibility to the institution. At this moment I am reaching for a particular kind of participatory style, one that Rosener (1990) defines as transformational, that is "getting subordinates to transform their own self-interest into the interest of the group through concern for a broader goal" (p. 120). The task at hand now also brings up the idea of power and its use. Zaleznik (1992) points out "leadership inevitably requires using power to influence the thoughts and actions of other people" (p. 26). I am aware that this lies ahead for me, but first there is the need for a pooling of thoughts, responses, hunches, and information. I am also aware of the need to be calm in the face of extensive unknowns and not to formulate plans too quickly. This capacity to tolerate lack of structure is one that I have learned to develop and appreciate.

At this time I must sort out and delete information, store some and save for later retrieval, very much like a computer. Part of a good intelligence system is to recognize what is important and also how much information I must give to others if I expect them to participate in making decisions. Another information guideline is to realize that no one has all the answers, and indeed, as in this instance, no one seems to have any answers, just a mass of random information.

While I have fluctuating degrees of apprehension and anxiety at this time, I also have a conviction and belief in the value of the social work product, and this optimism I try to convey to the staff. I cannot offer extended reassurance that everything will work out, I can reassure that the department remains supportive of each and every worker, and the work that we do.

Lastly, I come to consider strategy and vision two key leadership concepts. Moltke, Bismarck's most successful commander, emphasized two important characteristics for the superior strategist: the ability to understand the significance of events without being influenced by current opinion, changing attitudes and one's own prejudice; and secondly, the ability to make decisions quickly without being deterred by perceived dangers (Hinterhuber and Popp, 1992). This unique process of close connection and cool detachment is also found in the recent article on "strategic stretch" (Hamel and Prahalad, 1993) which advocates that the single most important task senior management faces is to create a fit between aspirations and resources.

This underscores the importance of vision. In many ways my vision of the effective, reflective, and compassionate worker has been realized, but will this vision mesh with unknown resources and models of care that will come about? Once more, looking back holds the key to the fuller visions and strategies that will evolve. The needs of patients caught in the morass of social, economic and medical systems were the original propelling force for social workers in health care in the very beginning. More than ever those needs and the common human needs that Charlotte Towle (1945) defined five decades ago persist today. The strengths of the social work product–the skill in mediating systems, in advocating for entitlements, in assessing the biopsychosocial needs of our patients and families in primary, secondary and tertiary care–are more relevant today to patients and to the institution. That some emphases may change; some patterns in staffing may change; and other structural rearrangements may be necessary, seems an obvious conclusion. To hospital management we must appear flexible and creative and collaborative. It makes no sense to create another strata of coordinating managers for new systems when social work experts are on hand. We must be rededicated as together we make new alliances in the helping process. To our staff we must communicate in a thoughtful and supportive manner, reassuring their professional integrity, but preparing for possible variations and changes in assignments, and practice emphases.

CONCLUSIONS

So I end as I began on a mixed militaristic and humanistic note. I believe I have come a long way in leadership, and the journey has been exhilarating, thus far. I have been effective in maintaining departmental strengths and alliances; in expanding directions, especially in research and personnel standards for excellence in practice in an academic setting; in improving communication between staff and management in both formal and informal ways. Recognizing my debt to the leaders first espoused, I add that my own vision and clinical skills have been developed and utilized, and tested and expanded. I have learned an enormous amount about institutional policy and administration and basic managerial principles and skills; and in addition to "hearing of voices" I have learned the values of fortitude and forbearance. As a leader I have also learned to value my own powers of reflection, but to grow in asserting my own decisions and directions, and for taking responsibility for them. In the decision making process I have learned to gather and sort and weigh information, as well as to store facts that don't mesh.

I have gained increasing skill in using others in the decision making process, but recognizing the importance of time limits. I have made alliances within and without the department, but I am comfortable with a necessary ultimate isolation.

I am most fortunate to have become a leader in an exciting and demanding setting that esteems both excellence and humanistic values in health care practice. My leadership space in time may not be in the optimism of the 50's and 60's or even the transition decades of the 70's or 80's, but rather what is now often termed an era of diminished expectations. I do not see this as bad luck, but rather a reality to which social work is well accustomed. Diminished resources, on a societal or personal scale, are serious and upsetting. I have no illusion that these crises necessarily harbor good luck or great opportunities, but they do demand active and creative leadership. The strengths that so fundamentally reside in both the profession of social work and the institution of which I am part, make that leadership all the more vital and invigorating.

REFERENCES

Austin, Michael J. (1989). Executive entry: Multiple perspectives on the process of muddling through. *Administration in Social Work, 13*, (3/4), 55-71.

Baker, Russell. (1993, April 3). Serving humble pie. *The New York Times*, sec. A. p. 15.

Hamel, Gary and Prahalad, C.K. (1993, March-April). Strategy as stretch and leverage. *Harvard Business Review*, pp. 75-84.

Hinterhuber, H. and Popp, W. (1992, Jan.-Feb.). Are you a strategist or just a manager? *Harvard Business Review*, pp. 105-113.

Roberts, Wess. (1993). *Leadership secrets of Attila the Hun*. New York: Warner Books.

Rosenberg, Gary.(1987). The social worker as manager in health care settings: An Experiential view, *Social Work in Health Care, 12*,(3), 71-84.

Rosenberg, Gary and Weissman, Andrew. (1981). Marketing social services in health care facilities. *Health and Social Work 6*,(3), 13-20.

Rosener, Judy B. (1990, Nov.-Dec.). Ways women lead. *Harvard Business Review*, pp. 119-125.

Towle, Charlotte. (1957). *Common Human Needs*. (Rev. edition). New York: N.A.S.W.

Zalenik, Abraham. (1992, March-April). Managers and leaders: Are they different? *Harvard Business Review*, 126-135.

The Effective Health Care Social Work Director

Margaret Dimond, ACSW
Madelyne Markowitz, ACSW

INTRODUCTION

Acute care hospitals have undergone dramatic changes in service delivery and reimbursement in the last decade. The alteration in health care organizations is connected to dwindling profits. The financial crisis hospitals have endured has secondarily changed the power and growth of medical social work departments. The goals and services of social work in a hospital setting have been forced to demonstrate economic worth. Timely discharges within DRG guidelines, increasing worker productivity, attending to cost-benefit ratios of service provision, and generating revenues are now common expectations for a social work director (Patti & Ezell, 1988).

There is a direct correlation of decreased governmental and philanthropic funding and new challenges for social work administrators. Marketing social work expertise and positive impact on patient satisfaction is essential for departmental survival (Genkins, 1985). However, though success or failure of a department's goals is linked

Margaret Dimond is Assistant Administrator, Emergency Medicine, Henry Ford Hospital, 2799 West Grand Boulevard, Detroit, MI 48202. Madelyne Markowitz is affiliated with the Social Work Department as a Team Leader at Henry Ford Hospital.

[Haworth co-indexing entry note]: "The Effective Health Care Social Work Director." Dimond, Margaret, and Madelyne Markowitz. Co-published simultaneously in *Social Work in Health Care* (The Haworth Press, Inc.) Vol. 20, No. 4, 1995, pp. 39-59; and: *Social Work Leadership in Healthcare: Directors' Perspectives* (ed: Gary Rosenberg, and Andrew Weissman), The Haworth Press, Inc., 1995, pp. 39-59. Multiple copies of this article/chapter may be purchased from The Haworth Document Delivery Center [1-800-3-HAWORTH; 9:00 a.m. - 5:00 p.m. (EST)].

39

to its leader, there is not a plethora of literature to denote which personality types, or managerial styles will be most effective for buoying the survival of medical social work functions. Change is a necessity. If social work leaders wish to transform and mold service delivery, they need to study, examine and adjust all aspects of their operations (Dublin, 1989). Those operations must be in harmony with the strategic plans and goals of the organization.

HFH PRESENT OPERATIONS: A GENERAL OVERVIEW

Henry Ford Hospital is located in Detroit, Michigan. It is a 900 bed urban teaching institution, specializing in tertiary care. The hospital is part of a multi-health corporation, which includes two community hospitals, a psychiatric facility, a substance abuse facility, and two nursing homes. The Henry Ford Health System also has a business arm that operates a home care agency, a durable medical equipment company, and an HMO.

The hospital is managed in a business-like atmosphere at all levels. Managers are evaluated not only on professional competence, but on how well they met their previous year's budget. This broad orientation to the milieu of the hospital is essential in order to understand the priorities of the social work director, and the operational aspects of the department; "If social work services are to remain an integral aspect of health care delivery, social work administrators will need to develop expertise and skill in operating within the political arena of multihealth systems" (Kenney, 1990).

Currently, nurses and social workers are teamed to perform social work and discharge planning activities. The staff of the department has been dual discipline since 1986. The department operates on a combination of unit- and service-based assignments. The hospital, out-patient clinics, and suburban medical centers have social work coverage. However, the main emphasis within the hospital is discharge planning. The Social Work Department reports through an Assistant Administrator, who also has responsibility for Pastoral Care, EAP, Case Management for Frail Elderly Program, and the Emergency Medicine Department. The administrative reporting structure changed in 1991, when the Director of Social Work was promoted to Assistant Administrator. Prior to that time, the department reported to an Operations Vice President.

The current arrangement of reporting relationships is working well, as there is a familiarity of operations, personnel, and political dilemmas. The mentoring role between the Assistant Administrator and the new Director has proved a valuable orientation piece. The Director has some historical sense of process and problem development. She has also had the advantage of being versed first hand on some short-term priorities versus guessing at where to place her energies in the first six months of her tenure. Though the Administrator and Director have different interpersonal styles, there is agreement on operations priorities. "With a clear understanding of both your boss and yourself, you can usually establish a way of working together that fits both of you, that is characterized by unambiguous mutual expectations, and that helps both of you be more productive and effective . . . above all, a good working relationship with a boss accommodates differences in work style" (Gabarro, Kotler, 1987).

During the last five years, the Social Work Department has faced developmental and maintenance opportunities, as well as perceived and real threats. The department is currently comprised of over forty staff members. Despite fiscal reductions and hiring freezes, the staff has doubled in size since 1988. The staff number alone is only one indicator of other innovations, achievements, and visions. One could safely say that the department has been re-created to meet future expectations rather than only reacting to current demands. The transition from a department fraught with low morale and productivity to employee empowered decision making occurred by careful planning. Compromise, communication, and competent leadership were incremental ingredients to the re-tooled approach. However, it is difficult to claim a good outcome without first examining process changes (Deming, 1982). To exemplify process and operational change, key quality standards must be a priority. In explaining the case study of Henry Ford Hospital's Social Work transformation, the integral theme is quality improvement, increased employee satisfaction, and productivity (Walton, 1986).

The health care manager must make certain that all of her or his assigned human resources are providing the health care organization with premium productivity and high level perfor-

mance in a long-term mutually beneficial manner. This mutual
benefit should extend to every level of the organization. That
is to say, each employee should feel motivated by his or her
manager as well as satisfied with the opportunities for skills
development on the job; the manager should benefit from the
synergistic effect of an entire group of inspired professionals
working cohesively; and the organization should reap the
benefits of all professional contributions. (Lombardi, 1992)

The aforementioned quote is reminiscent of theory taught in
health care administration graduate courses. In reality, the state-
ments incorporate the vision and accomplishments gleaned in the
Department of Social Work at Henry Ford Hospital in the late 1980s
to present day operations. However, change is decidedly difficult
and tracing the historical events leading to change will be helpful
for a more complete understanding of the Henry Ford Hospital
experience.

BACKGROUND OF CHANGE

Both authors have been members of the Social Work Department
for a number of years. The first author began as a line staff on the
Neuro-Surgery Service, was promoted to supervisor in 1986, promoted to Director of Social Work in 1988, and now holds the
position of Assistant Administrator, with responsibility for the Social Work area. The second author has held both in- and out-patient
clinical positions, moved into an AIDS research-oriented position
in 1988, and was promoted to clinical team leader in 1991. She has
responsibility for supervising five specialty staff, and coordinating
the student internship program, which averages 15 graduate students per year. The authors are confident that they are gifted with
both survival skills and the flexibility to withstand political fire-
fights. It is the authors' belief that the transformation of the department must be traced to the late eighties, when staff were challenged
with unprecedented tasks which required flexibility and trust.

A change in management at the director's level in 1988 spurred
staff to a natural synergy for change. The previous director had
begun to bring the department past the post-1983 DRG shock

waves that began to emphasize accountability with discharge planning. In order to position the department for the rapid policy updates associated with organizational shifts, some operational decisions in social work were made without wide spread staff input. The changes were clearly made to advance the discharge planning function of the department (e.g., initiating referral boxes on each nursing unit). However, staff were ingrained in established habits and behaviors, thus felt somewhat threatened by practical work flow modifications. "What employees resist is usually not technical change, but social change–the change in their human relationships that generally accompanies technical change" (Lawrence, 1987).

Hence, employees perceived themselves as victims during an essential health care transformation process in the mid-1980s. Because conflict between employee views and management actions was a sporadic but recurrent theme, employee morale and the sense of teamwork was impacted.

> Conflict in the health care workplace can be a most damaging force when employees find a source of conflict and, in their collective perception, the manager does not resolve it quickly, resolutely, and clearly, the conflict can fester and hamper productivity and quality of care. (Lombardi, 1992)

Thus, in 1988 when management transition took place in the Social Work Department, employees were in need of an approach that encouraged teamwork, collaboration, and empowerment. The search was conducted for a new director, and the internal candidate was appointed. At the time of the promotion, it was obvious what not to do, and less clear how the department should be rejuvenated.

The first task of the new leadership was to establish credibility and vision with staff. "The function of supervision and the function of leadership are synonymous: empowering or influencing others to accomplish some organizational aim or goal" (Dublin, 1989). Until trust in leadership is established, staff will continue in a mode of distrust and will not engage in risk taking behavior to stray from established norms.

Staff focus groups were formed to elicit staff input on major issues, and problem solving approaches to resolve those issues. Staff were initially leery, and commented that their views wouldn't be taken seriously. However, utilizing quality methods to establish criteria for the focus group outcomes, and provision of education on flowcharting process change, proved useful to staff in terms of the seriousness of the project (Deming, 1982). Group priorities were presented in staff meetings following completion of the projects. The ideas were directly related to department operations (e.g., paperwork, caseload mix, staff cohesiveness). The ideas were transformed into departmental goals, and ultimately achieved within one year. The focus group achievements were the first step in the departmental transformation. "Managerial behaviors that have received empirical support for their contribution to worker performance include: the setting of objectives, feedback or knowledge of results, and worker participation in decision making" (Granvold, 1978).

The trend of employee participation was well received by staff, and ensuing operational decisions were patterned by a shared governance approach. Other departmental reporting relationships were conducted in a similar manner (e.g., EAP Program).

CORRELATION OF MANAGEMENT STYLE AND DEPARTMENTAL STRUCTURE

"The essential qualities of leadership and the acts that define a leader: the ability to hear what is left unspoken, humility, commitment, the value of looking at reality from many vantage points, the ability to create an organization that draws out the unique strengths of every member" (Kim, Mauborgne, 1992). The quote is a quintessential epitaph that every successful manager would like engraved on a retirement plaque. However, reality dictates that many people manage, few people lead.

Management philosophy and practice directly patterns day to day operations for a department. One only has to look at history to derive that an autocrat utilizes fear, a democrat operates on group buy-in. Participatory management, falling somewhere in the middle, solicits group input, but also takes the brunt of some needed executive decision-making consequences.

At Henry Ford Hospital, it seemed that the only management approach for the staff would be a tough yet encouraging one. Staff needed to begin setting goals for the future. The prerequisite to any significant departmental change was management of interpersonal conflict in the department, and promotion of positive morale. "The health care manager in a progressive organization must do more than employ a set of motivators and shared values to lead staff effectively toward desired goals. The manager must also manage the dynamics of conflict, change, and cultural differences to maximize staff performance" (Lombardi, 1992).

Nevermind who the department's internal and external customers were. Staff did not care about customers, or productivity, or any standard of care; their reactions were in the mode of self-protection, defensive and reactive interactions. Thus, the first task of the new leader was to: open communication, change the "low hanging fruit" problems, and to re-establish standards of care.

The philosophy employed was one of understanding the pain and frustration the staff felt, and providing action plans with measurable outcomes in short time frames to address the frustration. "Management must feel pain and dissatisfaction with past performance, and must have the courage to change" (Deming, 1982). Group participation led to venting, healing, and eventually planning for the department's destiny.

In a methodical manner, the department structure was transformed to incorporate a shared governance concept. The essence of shared governance is shared decision making and employee empowerment. Several standing committees were created to address central operational procedures and problems. Examples of some committees are: documentation, community liaison, early discharge initiatives, and quality improvement. The committees were a resounding success, and served to promote change that was employee driven. "As they work together to improve quality, workers and management build mutual respect and trust" (Scholtes, 1988).

The present structure is affiliated with the now popular quality theories. Change and process improvement begin with those closest and most knowledgeable to the process. Essentially, it is a paradigm shift from "top down" decision making to "bottom up" collaboration. The director no longer dictates protocol; rather, he or she coaches the staff to create and maintain protocol; if this task can be achieved, then increased employee quality of work, productivity and efficiency will be accomplished (Walton, 1986).

Within two years of establishing a committee structure, and creating teams in the department, several measurable outcomes were traced. Using the departmental information system, and quality assurance monitors, data was compiled on: increased productivity, decreased discharge delays, increased patient/physician satisfaction with social work services, and increased staff satisfaction with their jobs.

To say that the transformation was not labor intensive would be false. However, the work in the short term facilitated payoff in the long term. "Where once there may have been barriers, rivalries, and distrust, the quality company fosters teamwork and partnerships with the workforce and their representatives" (Scholtes, 1988). To establish solid goals and lead staff to achieve those goals is the vision to see a future, and the political and emotional strength to create the roadmap of change complete with data to substantiate the positive outcomes. Once change can be achieved, the opportunities are endless. Staff education, departmental collaboration, research, and innovative programming were the benefits realized by the Henry Ford Social Work staff, after some painful growth.

ORIENTATION, SUPERVISION AND CONTINUING EDUCATION

Initially, the Social Work and Discharge Planning Department orientation program was sketchy and haphazard. It often consisted of the newly hired social worker beginning to intervene with patients within the first few days of employment. Departmental orientation for new social workers and discharge planners evolved into a uniform program that takes approximately two months to complete. The social work director, in collaboration with new and experienced line staff, developed this program.

> The general competence of new social work entrants to health care settings may be viewed with some suspicion; that is, the degree to which they have been educated and prepared in schools of social work to assure a professional role in a spe-

cialized area may certainly be questioned. There is a continuing tension between social work education which for years has stressed the production of generalist practitioners able to operate at a beginning level of professional competence in a wide range of settings, and, for example, social work administrators of organizations charged with delivering health care services. The latter would like to see the development of more specialized forms of social work education or, failing that, the introduction of post degree residency programmes. (Erickson & Erickson; 1990)

To assist the new employee in developing an understanding of the system they are entering, a set of orientation programs is provided for them to attend and experience. At the time the new entrant is offered the position, he/she is given a pre-orientation manual that was developed by line staff. The new employee has two to four weeks prior to starting to ingest the major policies and procedures (documentation, dress code, attendance). The new entrant initially attends the hospital sponsored day long orientation that highlights hospitalwide policies, programs and procedures. Upon completion of this process the departmental orientation begins.

The individual's supervisor guides them through the department orientation process. This orientation instructs new social workers and discharge planners about departmental expectations, policies, and procedures. It introduces them to other hospital departments that the social work department often collaborates with (Risk, Utilization, Nursing). Core competencies are the basis of this program and are fundamental to ones functioning successfully as a professional social worker within the Henry Ford Health System. The core competencies include understanding the structure, function and operations of the department, documentation standards, quality assurance activities, clinical service assignments, interdepartmental relationships and community services. The orientation program involves line staff participation in acclimating the new employee. Line staff may teach the new worker about documentation standards, acclimating them to their hospital floor and staff, and community resources. Staff participation is imperative because it encourages peer support that helps the new worker in adjusting to the department and the hospital system that is often overwhelming. At the point of employment the staff member is given a 90 day contract that outlines essential learning tasks during the orientation period. Each task has a time-line (visit local rehabilitation unit within one month). At the end of the probationary period, the employee signs the contract with his or her supervisor. The employee then completes a confidential satisfaction survey on the orientation. The survey is routed to the department's quality assessment committee.

SUPERVISION

Supervision occurs regularly and in a variety of methods within the social work department. Traditional supervision is available to the individual depending upon their needs and interests. Practice issues, counseling skills, systems problems and the professional growth goals are the basis of supervision. As a group, the social work and discharge planning supervisors practice an "open door policy" modeled by the director. Therefore, should a worker experience a problem requiring immediate attention, someone in management is readily available. As Richard A. Dublin noted "Supervisors can empower and lead staff to accomplish the work of the organization, while ensuring the quality of services provided by the agency" (Dublin, 1989).

Supervision is based on several concepts that provide direction and structure, the learning process for staff. Many of the concepts are as outlined below:

> Requisite activities and task for effective supervision that take into account concern for task, for people, and for competitive job orientations have been identified as: (a) setting individual and group objectives for task allocation and implementation; (b) implementing shared decision making; (c) directing group process (including agenda building); (d) planning work and case management; (e) developing communication networks; (f) evaluating performance; (g) motivating workers; (h) case consultation and professional support; (i) team building; (j) worker and client advocacy; (k) conflict management; and (l) planned change at dyadic, team, and intergroup levels with particular attention to

coalescing separate interests on behalf of employees and clients. (Cohen, Rhodes, 1977)

These considerations were taken into account when developing the various modes of supervision for department staff including the managers.

Group supervision is available to social workers and discharge planners through their team. Teams, composed of four to five individuals working in similar hospital units, meet weekly to discuss their case loads, scheduling issues, and broader departmental concerns. During team meetings staff members often discuss problematic cases and wider system concerns examining the various problems involved and methods or interventions that may be employed to resolve them. "Staff members can present a particular issue to the staff group for advice. When colleagues offer suggestions, they are actually helping themselves with similar concerns while providing help to the individual. This is one of the most important dynamics in mutual aid groups: participants are getting help for themselves when they provide it to a colleague" (Shulman, 1993).

STAFF EDUCATION

"Health settings are learning settings, and in view of rapidly changing knowledge and technologies, everyone is a life-long learner" (Erickson, R., Erickson, G. 1989). Continuing education is important in keeping a social work department current and a vital player in today's changing health care marketplace. Harris and Allison describe principles guiding departmental education opportunities. Harris and Allison's principles are as follows: "(1) educational opportunities should be available that relate to each social worker's specific learning needs and are appropriate to his or her level of training and experience. (2) educational opportunities in an agency should provide a formal means for social workers to broaden their knowledge about health care issues through exposure to colleagues in different specialties" (Harris, Allison, 1982). The principles are incorporated into Henry Ford Hospital's Department of Social Work's educational programs.

At Henry Ford Hospital continuing education occurs on multiple levels and in a variety of methods. Within the Social Work Department education occurs at least twice a month during scheduled staff meetings. One of the two meetings is Journal Club, an institution within the department and hospital. During Journal Club, a staff member presents a topic of interest and an accompanying article. The discussant highlights salient points and encourages didactic interaction with staff.

The Staff Development Committee within the Social Work Department is comprised of staff members from the department. Their charge is maintaining clinical education for the staff. The staff development committee surveys the department yearly to ascertain interests and needs. The survey solicits what educational components must be developed for the department's continuing education. Speakers from the department, the hospital, and community are invited to lecture on a variety of topics of staff interest. Topics have included Transference/Counter-transference, Chemical Dependency in the Elderly, Chronic Illness and the family. Attendance at staff meetings has increased since the Staff Development committee began exploring the department's educational needs and interests.

Within the hospital there are a variety of means of accessing continuing education. Many Medical Divisions and Departments within the Henry Ford Health System open their Journal Clubs (Psychiatry, Infectious Diseases, Oncology) to interested hospital staff, often sending advance announcements of topics and speakers. Medical Grand Rounds are open to all hospital staff with topics ranging from specific diseases and treatment modalities to exploration of biomedical ethics. Staff is encouraged to attend meetings such as Ethics for Lunch, the Employee Assistance Program lecture series, and other similar programs.

Within the Detroit metropolitan community there are two medical schools and several colleges. Staff of the social work department are advised to attend lectures that they feel will enhance their practice skills at the university level or through many agencies sponsoring programs. Joining professional groups and attending their meetings enhances networking and education. Therefore, interested staff members are encouraged to pursue this activity.

Management recommends that line staff with expertise in specific areas share that knowledge with others by lecturing and publishing.

Staff can use the hospital's medical library for literature searches and work on research projects either within the department, locally or nationally. Some staff have felt the need to develop special groups to fulfill educational and practice voids for themselves and colleagues. To this end, two staff members began a support and education group that meets monthly to aid their peers coping with loss and grief in their daily work with patients and families.

> Social work is an interactional profession, which means that the subject of our work is the internal process of the person in relation to the external behavior; the person in relation to external system; and systems in relation to systems. The interactional nature of the profession and of the process with which we work is ever changing, which mandates continued study, analysis, and education. (Dublin, 1989)

GRADUATE INTERNSHIP PROGRAM

Until the late 1980s the Department of Social Work had little involvement with student education because of lack of commitment to the field supervision process. Yet it became much more difficult to hire social workers with experience in health care settings.

> A major current concern of both social work educators and practitioners in health care settings is the difficulty in attracting the most highly qualified MSW social work graduates to jobs in health care settings and retaining them once they are hired. There has been a marked decrease in the numbers of those who choose hospital based or other health related agencies as their first option. (Mailick, 1991)

A compounding factor was the lack of interest in coming to an inner city urban facility, when the compensation and salary is similar to homogeneous suburban community facilities.

The Henry Ford Hospital Social Work Department developed a collaborative relationship with Wayne State University's School of Social Work. It became noticeable that the school did not have a health care concentration that addressed the educational requirements of medical social workers. The Social Work Department and the school of Social Work collaborated in developing the core competencies defining what students should master during their internships. Currently, the department accepts an average of fifteen graduate level students for field placement a year.

The Social Work Department's orientation program instructs students about hospital and departmental policies, procedures and expectations over a two week period. Lectures and exercises cover concrete tasks and clinical skills (counseling techniques, first interviews, grief work). The student coordinator facilitates the orientation, yet most of the social work and discharge planning staff participates in instructing the students. During orientation, the students "shadow" their field instructor to ascertain how a hospital social worker intervenes with patients, families, physicians and ancillary staff. The students go into the community, visiting a nursing home and go on a home care visit with a visiting nurse. Each student receives a Student Orientation Manual that contains articles and exercises they complete during their training period. Rauch found that the benefits of helping students to begin hospital field placement through an active learning approach are several. The clearly defined structure aids in reducing anxiety; students' active involvement achieves more effective learning of initial information; self-direction enables feelings of mastery and competence (Rauch, 1984).

Students and field instructors are matched according to interests and availability of the medical service. Change of placement is an option for the students and field instructors at the end of each semester. Much discussion occurs before this process to ensure satisfaction of the student and the field instructor. Placements are available on hospital units, a variety of ambulatory care clinics, the emergency room, and in the community with the Henry Ford Hospital Home Care agency and the Care Management for the Elderly. Utilizing this approach enables students to experience medical social work and its ability to provide care in a multiplicity of settings and along a continuum.

> The areas of satisfaction affected by provision of training in multiple methods suggest that assignment to more than one method furthers both educational and organizational goals . . .

training in multiple methods may be a comparatively strong strategy for enhancing student satisfaction through program design. Positive correlations between consortia participation and student satisfaction suggest that such participation may be a cost effective as well as educationally effective means of strengthening learning opportunities in hospital programs. (Showers, 1990)

The students participate in their Journal Club and Brown Bag Lunch meetings. During the Journal Club, various social work staff members facilitate a discussion with the students about topics of interest to both. Discussion topics include psychosocial aspects of transplantation, loss and grief, and crisis intervention techniques of Emergency Medicine social work. During the brown bag luncheons, students address many of their concerns. This year the students are employing a system's approach to their units and casework. The student coordinator participates in the brown bag lunches with the goal of listening to the student concerns, facilitating discussion and incorporating suggestions into this program.

Quality assurance occurs twice a year in the student program. When the students finish the orientation program they complete a questionnaire regarding their satisfaction with the program on various levels (lectures, manual, visits in community). The second quality assurance survey occurs before the students complete the program and leave the facility. This questionnaire queries satisfaction with supervision, brown bag and journal club, unit placement, teaching materials and so forth. The process of the internship program is improved based upon the student's responses.

The student coordinator believes staff participation in this program is imperative to its success. The students need to see the variety of social work's roles within the hospital setting to appreciate the diversity and importance of medical social work. Through diverse experiences the student integrates a multifaceted view of medical social work and may opt for selecting a medical setting upon graduation from school. We have been successful during the last four years in recruiting new graduates into Henry Ford Health System.

Findings suggest that social work students in hospitals simultaneously experience both higher levels of stress and higher levels of satisfaction with field work than do students placed in other settings. Student satisfaction can have organizational as well as educational implications for hospital social work departments. Field education gives providers a pool of known job applicants trained in organizational policies, procedures, and philosophy. High satisfaction levels presumably make it more likely that students will remain as employees. Further, organizations gaining a reputation for providing quality field education will attract high-caliber students and the most competent graduates. (Showers, 1990)

COLLABORATIVE NETWORKS

Collaborative networks exist within health care institutions and in every local community. External networks are vital to hospital social work departments' viability with resource linkage. Collaboration with internal and external resource pools is critical in hospitals whose demographics limit diverse case mix and payors. At Henry Ford Hospital, internal collaboration occurs for a variety of reasons. Several social work positions were created during times of hospital downsizing. The new funding sources were supplied by medical services or grants. Social work staff demonstrated the need for additional staffing by collecting data from the Social Work Information Management Systems. The data highlighted a positive correlation of increased length of stay with decreased social work interventions. Through intensive lobbying with medical staff and administration, positions were created in both the ambulatory clinics and in-patient units.

Health care social workers function in a host or secondary setting. That is, the primary function of health care services has usually been directed to biomedical concerns, and other services (including social work) exist as a supplement to medical care. There has been increasing pressure to develop truly collaborative teams where the physician would be the "bio-medical specialist as part of (a) primary care team, appreciative of the psychosocial and social dimensions but not inexpertly attempting to provide them. The notion of a collaborative, rather than co-operative, health care team is appealing to those professional groups whose expertise seems often neglected by physicians. (Erickson, R., Erickson, G. 1989)

Several staff members participate on quality improvement teams that are examining the needs of patients with the goal of improving service to patients. The quality improvement teams are multi-disciplinary and have members from various departments throughout the Henry Ford Health System. One team developed a short term stay program for patients undergoing hip replacement surgery that addresses the patient's psychosocial issues regarding surgery, pain and discharge planning needs. Another team is exploring the needs of HIV patients and proposing a system-wide case management program.

Fund raising is an important and fun project for the staff. The money raised is used for the prescriptions and medical supplies for patient's who cannot afford to fill their prescriptions. Staff efforts have included bake sales, white elephant items, Tupperware® and cosmetic sales. Other departments have held sales donating proceeds to the Emergency Medication fund. Recently the Corporate Philanthropy Department committed their skills to the project because the demand has out-grown the supply and administration is aware of the imperative nature of the fund.

Internal collaboration is extended in Henry Ford Hospital to include line staff working on multiple committees. The committees are hospital wide which afford social work staff systems perspective in decision making. Some committees in 1992 where social work played a big role include the Human Rights Committee (Institutional Review Board), the Institutional Biomedical Ethics Committee, the Cancer Coordinating Committee, Senior Services Committee and the Utilization Management Committee.

COMMUNITY OUTREACH

Emphasis on community collaboration has increased since the mid-1980s. Initially the hospital's attitude was one of being an "island" within the local community. There was little outreach into the community "to give back" to the neighborhoods or agencies. The philosophy was that the institution did not need to reach out or work with others. As economic times changed, the hospital's attitude softened. The Chief Operating Officer realized that government funding and programming was moving into the community. This required a change in the social work departments program planning too. It became necessary to work with agencies in the community to bridge skills, resources and alliances. Alliances began to be built with agencies working with the elderly, people with HIV disease, and other populations with special needs. In 1989, the hospital administrator developed an urban initiative task force to address community relations. Social work played a key role in the development and implementation of the task force objectives.

Henry Ford Hospital's Social Work Department felt a strong commitment to the community in which its resides. This is demonstrated in several ways by staff members. The department worked toward developing programs that serve the community. The Care Management Program for the Frail Elderly proves this commitment. This program provides a continuum of care to area homebound seniors with the goal of sustaining the elderly at home. A BSW and a RN staff the program and are responsible for home assessments and referrals to community resources. The Care Management staff must stay active in the community. This preserves their knowledge base on area resources and perpetuates their working relationship with community based agencies.

Another crucial area that has required community outreach is AIDS. Community outreach in this area began eight years ago with the goal of learning about and developing resources to serve the HIV (+) community. The department's role then was to define patient care needs within the hospital and explore whether this was the same throughout the community. Through the effort of the AIDS social worker, strong ties were cultivated in the Detroit metropolitan area that helped in providing care to people with HIV disease. Community outreach from hospitals was not common nor encouraged during that time. Resources for discharge needs or emotional support did not exist in our community. Therefore community outreach aided the patients and our department by joining agencies to create services until traditional ones became available. Staff became involved in the training and education of AIDS community based agency personnel (case managers). The social work director facilitated developing and implementing quality assurance monitors in an AIDS case management agency to ascertain the level of performance of their line staff and the services provided to their clients.

Staff members developed the "Adopt a Family Program" seven years ago. The purpose of the program is to link departments with needy families during the holidays. The program begins in September when line staff identify patients and families from their caseload that could use assistance during the holidays. Departments throughout the hospital "Adopt a Family" and provide food and gifts for them on Thanksgiving or Christmas. This has grown significantly and is now a departmental and hospital tradition. It's encouraging in how the program brings hospital staff together for several months.

RESEARCH

"The increasing demand for social work research is putting the entire profession on notice that the direction of health care delivery is changing and consequently the profession must come up with creative as well as practical solutions to its problems" (Taylor, 1989). Research in the Department of Social Work and Discharge Planning occurs both informally and formally. Informal research is on-going in the quality assurance programs that are constantly performed in our department. Quality assurance monitors collect data regarding caseload size, case acuity, patient demographics, resource utilization, documentation standards and so forth. Quality assurance audits generate data that is useful for research and grant proposals.

To encourage participation in research, a research task force was developed to educate staff members regarding the "how to's." The Journal Club helps bolster staff's knowledge and interest in research by promoting new ideas in the field. These are only a couple of the techniques E.P. Simon recommended in her article "Research for the Research Phobic" for helping staff overcome research anxiety and encourage staff to become involved (Simon, 1991).

Academic research has begun in the department in the last few years. The latest project was collaborative on a national level with other social workers within the National Institutes of Health, National Institute of Allergy and Infectious Disease's Terry Beirn Community Program for Clinical Research on AIDS (TBCPCRA). The research project investigated the perceptions of community advisory board members whether they influence local and national program planning and AIDS protocol development.

Many staff papers are written or presented at local, state, national and international meetings. The authors are often supported by medical staff if their work involves travel given budgetary restraints that influence the social work department. Research is being further explored and encouraged by departmental staff through the research task force. Areas of exploration include the ability to collaborate with local schools of social work.

CONCLUSION

It is sometimes difficult to look within one's departmental operations for advice for colleagues, or to claim successes. Every department of social work in health care has positive aspects, and opportunities for change. It is the authors' hope that the Henry Ford Hospital experience can exemplify the excitement and challenge of change. The future of medical social work will necessitate directors to promote quality outcomes, economic worth, expertise, and innovations. Collaboration, negotiating politics, and igniting a positive environment of change will be key quality expectations of social work administrators in the next decade (Deming, 1982). Are we prepared for the challenge?

REFERENCES

Allison, Mary Ann and Allison, Eric; *Managing Up, Managing Down*: A Fireside Book, Simon and Schuster, New York, NY, 1986.

Cohen, Neil A., Ph.D., Rhodes, Gary B., MSW; "Social Work Supervision: A View Toward Leadership Style and Job Orientation in Education and Practice," *Administration in Social Work*; Fall 1977.

Deming, W. Edward; *Out of Crisis*, Massachusetts Institute of Technology Center for Advanced Engineering Study, Cambridge, MA, 1982.

Dublin, Richard A; "Supervision and Leadership Styles," Social Casework: The Journal of Contemporary Social Work, December 1989.

Erickson, Rebecca, and Erickson, Gerald; "An Overview of Social Work Practice in Health Care Settings," *Social Work Practice in Health Care Settings*, Canadian Scholar's Press, Toronto, Canada, 1989.

Gabarro, John J., Kotter, John P.; "Managing Your Boss," *People: Managing Your Most Important Asset*, Harvard Business Review, Boston, MA, 1987.

Genkins, Mary; "Strategic Planning for Social Work Marketing," *Administration in Social Work*, The Haworth Press, Inc., Spring 1985.

Granvold, Donald K, Ph.D.; "Supervision By Objectives," *Administration in Social Work*, Haworth Press, Summer 1978.

Harris, Dorothy V., Allison, Elizabeth Keith, "Performance Management and Professional Development as Separate Functions of Supervision," *Health and Social Work*; 1982.

Kenney, John J.; "Social Work Management in Emergency Health Care Systems," *Health and Social Work*, February 1990.

Kim, W. Chan, Mauborgne, Reneè A.; "Parables of Leadership," Harvard Business Review, Boston, MA, July-August 1992.

Lawrence, Paul R., "How to Deal With Resistance to Change," *People: Managing Your Most Important Asset*, Harvard Business Review, Boston, MA, 1987.

Lombardi, Donald, Ph.D.; Progressive Health Care Management Strategies, American Hospital Association, Chicago, IL, 1992.

Mailick, Mildred D., DSW; "Recruitment and Retention of MSW Graduates," *Social Work in Health Care*, 1991.

Patti, Reno J., DSW, Ezell, Mark, Ph.D.; "Performance Priorities and Administrative Practice in the Hospital Social Work Department," *Social Work in Health Care*, 1988.

Rauch, Julia B., Ph.D.; "Helping Students to Begin Hospital Field Placements: An Active Learning Approach," *Social Work in Health Care*, Spring 1984.

Scholtes, Peter R.; *The Team Handbook: How to Use Teams to Improve Quality*, Joiner Associates, Madison, WI, 1988.

Showers, Nancy; "Hospital Graduate Social Work Field Work Programs: A Study in New York City," *Health and Social Work*, February 1990.

Shulman, Lawrence; *Interactional Supervision*, NASW Press, Washington, D.C., 1993.

Simon, Ellen Perlman; "Research for the Research Phobic: Developing Research Expertise in Hospital Social Work," *Health and Social Work*, National Association of Social Workers, Inc., vol. 16, no. 2, May 1991.

Taylor, Patricia; "New Wave Social Work: Practice Roles for the 1990's and Beyond," *Social Work Practice in Health Care Settings*, Canadian Scholar's Press, Toronto, Canada, 1989.

Walton, Mary; "The Deming Management Method," Perigee Books, New York, NY, 1986.

The Effective Healthcare
Social Work Director:
Managing the Social Work Department
at Beth Israel Hospital

Jane B. Mayer, LICSW

For the past five years I have been Director of the Social Work
Department at Boston's Beth Israel Hospital, and Clinical Instructor, Department of Social Medicine and Health Policy, Harvard
Medical School. First and foremost, this position entails managing
and leading a staff of 58, including Masters prepared clinical social
workers, community resource specialists (BSW's), and administrative support staff, plus twelve trainees (social work interns and
post-master's fellows). In managing and leading a Department of
this size, my continuing challenge has been to ensure excellence in
patient care services while at the same time providing a stimulating,
supportive work environment that offers multiple, fulfilling opportunities for staff and enhances professional social work development. This is not an innovative concept at Beth Israel Hospital.
Since 1928 when Ms. Ethel Cohen pioneered the Social Work Department, efforts have focused on growth and innovation both in
service and in academics. My predecessors carried the mantle; as do

Jane B. Mayer is Director of the Social Work Department, Beth Israel Hospital, 330 Brookline Avenue, Boston, MA 02215, and Clinical Instructor, Department of Social Medicine and Health Policy, Harvard Medical School.

[Haworth co-indexing entry note]: "The Effective Healthcare Social Work Director: Managing the
Social Work Department at Beth Israel Hospital." Mayer, Jane B. Co-published simultaneously in
Social Work in Health Care (The Haworth Press, Inc.) Vol. 20, No. 4, 1995, pp. 61-72; and: *Social Work
Leadership in Healthcare: Directors' Perspectives* (ed: Gary Rosenberg, and Andrew Weissman),
The Haworth Press, Inc., 1995, pp. 61-72. Multiple copies of this article/chapter may be purchased from
The Haworth Document Delivery Center [1-800-3-HAWORTH; 9:00 a.m. - 5:00 p.m. (EST)].

© 1995 by The Haworth Press, Inc. All rights reserved.

I. Many of the programs detailed in this paper are the product of my efforts and the efforts of my predecessors to maintain a productive, vigorous Department with high performance expectations in a creative work environment.

CENTRAL MISSION

The Beth Israel Hospital is a 504-bed, acute care teaching hospital of Harvard Medical School. Its Social Work Department is a clinical department with primary responsibility for the care of psychological and social problems presented by the Hospital's patients and their families. As described in the Department's mission statement, "The delivery of direct patient care services is foremost in our work. Assessment and treatment of psychosocial problems is considered an inherent component of adequate health care to aid patients and families in adjusting to their illness and hospitalization" (Mission Statement, 1992). Our interventions run the gamut of clinical social work services and include: direct short and/or long term treatment (alone or in groups), case management, crisis intervention, advocacy, and community liaison.

Additionally, the development of an optimal discharge plan has always been a significant social work function in the department. Skilled discharge planning is essential to smooth hospital management as well as to patient well-being. Therefore, the social work staff collaborate with all hospital departments toward the goal of returning a patient to his/her community at maximum functioning.

OTHER DEPARTMENTAL FUNCTIONS
AND STAFF DEVELOPMENT

The Social Work Department has a long history of training social work students from various graduate schools of social work. Several staff have also taught policy, casework, and social work practice at the local graduate social work schools. Since training and education figure prominently among the criteria for advancement, the Department also offers post-graduate fellowship training programs in Oncology Social Work and Gerontology Social Work, two key areas of specialization. The Masters program and post-Masters program have their own unique curriculum and learning expectations. For example, social work interns have, in addition to individual supervision, seminars in general health care issues, domestic violence, clinical case conference, and an informal student "lunch," whereas the Fellowship training programs offer flexibility for the adult learner who has particular learning expectations and needs. Fellows must write and present a scholarly paper at the conclusion of their program.

Opportunities for staff supervision are based on competency, performance reviews, and training coordinator evaluations. Staff supervision usually comes after a social worker has gained proficiency in supervising social work interns. And, with developing supervisory and administrative expertise, a clinical social worker can advance the career ladder from a Social Worker I to a senior supervisor (Social Worker III), to a Division Chief.

There are numerous other educational opportunities within the Department, such as a ten-series Grand Rounds program and five to seven continuing education courses per academic year. The content of these educational programs emerges from a staff educational needs assessment administered each spring. Courses are relevant to Departmental practice and include timely issues of managed care, violence in the family, AIDS, etc. Additionally a "Topics in Aging" Seminar, developed as an extension of the post-graduate training program in gerontology, is open to all staff.

Three other major staff opportunities enhance social work development. First, for the last several years, the Beatrice Phillips Sachs Writing Award has encouraged staff to write and publish professional articles. Staff and alumnae submit professional papers which are peer reviewed, with a winner selected annually. The winner presents his/her paper at an award ceremony and receives a certificate, a cash prize, and a dinner in his/her honor. To further encourage the development of writing skills, the Department hires a professional writer to coach staff in writing. Many of the papers written since the inception of this program have been published and delivered at our Grand Rounds series, Grand Rounds series at neighboring hospitals, and professional conferences.

Second is an educational exchange program with hospital social workers in Melbourne, Australia. This highly acclaimed program enables a Beth Israel Hospital social worker to spend one month in Australia exploring a particular area of professional interest. Participating staff have examined areas such as the community mental health delivery system, AIDS care, and the development of clinical group work programs. Likewise, Australian social workers visiting Beth Israel Hospital have learned about our quality improvement program, supervisory system, oncology and renal transplant programs. Upon return, social workers write-up and present their experience at a staff meeting. This popular program has had a major impact on participants as it is rare that staff are able to spend this much time, at no cost to them, learning about an area of interest.

Third, the Social Work Department has developed faculty ties to Harvard Medical School. Several staff have the opportunity to teach the required Patient/Doctor course in the medical students' first and third years. The course blends patient-student interactions, written cases, and student projects as they relate to social, economic, and ethical issues that affect the patient-doctor relationship. This teaching opportunity affords social work staff the chance to have an impact on medical education in areas that are critical to our profession.

Research has not received as much attention as other Departmental functions. Over the past five years research has included collaboration with both local family service agencies and physician funded research. For example, the Department received a large grant to train family members of frail elders living at home to serve as case managers. Evaluation of the effectiveness of the training program and post-test comparisons revealed that the experimental group family members performed significantly more case management tasks on behalf of their elderly relatives than did family members in the control group (Mayer, 1990).

Currently two social work staff participate in a grant-sponsored multidisciplinary group effort to examine the role of physicians in knowing about patient risks for adverse medical outcomes. This group is creating a statistical model to predict adverse patient outcomes such as death and readmission.

Realizing the importance of accurate, accessible data to facilitate research, the Social Work Department is revising its statistical data gathering to more accurately reflect interventions, patient outcomes, and acuity.

To encourage future research, the Department has proposed the development of an annual award to recognize research projects that contribute to and expand the knowledge base of social work practice and promote a deeper understanding of the profession. Acceptable proposals might include, but are not limited to, evaluation of a particular clinical practice or training program, a descriptive study, an exploratory study, or application of certain research findings. Along with a cash prize, the award will also fund the consultation fee of a social work researcher, including data collection and statistical analysis time.

COMMUNITY AND COLLEGIAL RELATIONS

The Social Work Department supports a broad definition of community to include the neighboring residential area, the Jewish community which financially supports the hospital, the professional social work community, and the inner-city neighborhoods that do not border the Hospital but have been historically tied to the Hospital for high-risk patient care.

Staff involvement in community activities in human service agencies, and/or professional organizations is encouraged. For example, several staff, including the Director, sit on Community and Professional Boards, such as the Visiting Nurse Association, NASW, and the Boston Children's Service. Staff also volunteer their time to speak at community centers, nursing homes, and hospice programs.

Many staff spend time in community training and education. Some participate in formal training or "mini-Residency" programs where, for example, community social workers learn the clinical issues around HIV spectrum diseases and the intravenous drug abuse population in a medical setting. Others participate in educational programs organized for community social workers in local nursing homes to learn about issues of abuse with elders and the advanced directive legislation.

Another highly successful community education program is a video tape developed by the Department's Chief Social Worker for

Discharge Planning titled, "After the Hospital: What's Next?" The tape reflects what patients and families experience in the discharge planning process and emphasizes the partnership between the patient, healthcare providers, the hospital, and the community. The tape is available to local community groups for viewing.

The Department also manages a jointly run housing program in collaboration with other area social work departments. The program, "Room Away From Home" assists out-of-town patients and families with suitable lodging for extended stays in Boston while they are undergoing treatment.

At times the Department makes financial contributions to local community agencies as a demonstration of support and appreciation. Recently the Social Work Department contributed money to a local temporary housing program that was having severe financial problems and made a significant "start-up" contribution to a newly forming local lodging facility for adult cancer patients and their families.

Finally, the Department enjoys a close affiliation with several community health centers located in the urban, low-income areas of Boston. Staff work closely with colleagues at the health centers and occasionally offer consultation or expert advise in specialized areas of care and/or case management services.

DEPARTMENT COLLABORATION

Within the Hospital social workers at all levels have many opportunities to collaborate with their colleagues. Since Nursing is strong at Beth Israel Hospital, social work staff collaborate closely with all primary care nurses as well as with house officers. Regular patient care rounds are encouraged and both nurses and house officers attempt to attend. At the administrative, managerial level social work Division Chiefs, Assistant Director, and Director attempt to work closely, plan new programs, and problem solve with their Nursing Director colleagues and the Medical Chiefs of Service. The Chief Social Worker for Discharge Planning and the Department's Assistant Director also work closely with the Director of Quality Assurance/Quality Improvement and jointly conduct discharge rounds. The Assistant Director works regularly on special projects with the Head of Admitting, the Computer Information Center, and various other senior administrative staff. The Social Work Director and Assistant Director meet regularly with the Associate Vice-President for Nursing to problem solve and update Departmental information.

Presently senior social workers frequently attend Hospital planning meetings and problem solving sessions. This involvement however has been evolutionary. The Assistant Director, the Chief Social Worker for Discharge Planning, and the Director have diligently worked at quantifying the Department's statistical information to make it relevant to issues of acuity and discharge. The importance of social work services on the timely discharge of patients is continually stressed, as is the case for social work's contribution to the well being of patients, families, and the Hospital's ethos of a high-quality caring place to receive health care. As a result of these efforts, and because the Hospital is moving towards a participatory management approach in order to improve productivity and reduce costs, social work is now frequently brought into planning sessions to evaluate systems issues on, for example, the stroke service, length of stay, pre-admission and third-party payor problems, and a planning and implementation program for the new advanced directive and health care proxy.

MY MANAGEMENT ROLE AT BETH ISRAEL HOSPITAL

In 1974, I moved to Boston and accepted a position as Chief Social Worker for the mental health unit of a community health center operated by the Beth Israel Hospital. In the late 1970's, as funding in maternal and child health diminished, I made a lateral move within the Hospital and became Chief Social Worker of the Ambulatory Medical Specialty areas – an extremely diverse group of clinical social workers covering Hematology/Oncology, Neurosciences, Dialysis and Transplant, Emergency Unit and other ambulatory outpatient clinics. An excellent training ground, this position helped to inform me about Hospital policies, politics, and strengthened my commitment to the history and mission of the Social Work Department. During these years as Chief Social Worker, I was unconsciously preparing for the administrative and managerial demands that I would ultimately face as

Director. Years later, while interviewing for the position as Director of the Department, I realized the importance of negotiating for specific Department necessities such as: an Assistant Director's position, a Special Fund for Staff Education, a direct reporting relationship to the Hospital President, and a faculty appointment to Harvard Medical School for the Director.

Currently, I have a dual reporting relationship to both the Associate Director and the Hospital President. This dual reporting works extremely well, as long as I am cautious not to use it in a competitive, splitting fashion. I meet regularly with the Hospital Associate Director for day-to-day operational issues, including budget. Then, on a monthly basis, I meet with the Hospital President to discuss "macro" or planning issues, grant opportunities, medical school activities, and future directions for social work. As part of the Hospital's top management group, I attend regular monthly fiscal conferences and administrative meetings which discuss the pulse of the Hospital, budget, and new program initiatives. This information is then shared with my administrative, managerial group.

I am forever vigilant to hear of opportunities for social work while at the same time learning early about pressures for cost containment. Despite the extremely strong tradition of social work at Beth Israel Hospital, with mounting pressures from the outside and internal belt tightening one must be constantly alert to Hospital politics and constraints.

RECENT MANAGEMENT CHANGES

Two recent events have dramatically changed me and the structure and organization of the Department. First, staff morale seemed low at the same time as the Hospital was requesting budget reductions. In response, staff developed and distributed a questionnaire which evaluated our current practice, users of our service, and future practice areas. Concurrently, I proposed the elimination (by attrition) of a social work manager's position, having assessed that we were top heavy in administrative staff. According to Johnson and Berger, these were, " . . . cuts in the area that would do least damage to provision of service and to the integrity of the Department" (Johnson and Berger, 1990).

Results of the survey identified such problematic areas as a service model which did not meet practice issues; some small Units in the Department which tended to reduce flexibility, collaboration, and communication; longstanding tensions between clinical staff and management; Hospital budget reductions; perceived low quality of work life; and external systems (i.e., managed care) which placed pressures on existing practices. It seemed as though a new structure was needed to address these problems. As a Department we then developed standards for making decisions about reorganization. These included: high quality patient care as our primary focus; balanced budgets and balanced caseloads a second consideration; and quality of work life (i.e., time for professional development and job security) the third factor. We reviewed significant Hospital data including occupancy rates, patient discharges, outpatient visits, etc., believing that "Awareness of hospital trends and events gives clearer understanding of the context in which change is to occur" (Johnson and Berger, 1990). We also evaluated all social work job descriptions paying close attention to roles and responsibilities. Ultimately we made some dramatic changes in the manager's job description.

As the planning meetings came to an end, we drew up a list of overarching principles for the new structure that included in addition to excellent patient care: consistent standards of practice, clarity in roles and responsibilities, a clear chain of command, Units of livable size with common patient care issues, adaptability to change, attention to staff needs, and some fun.

In the midst of the planning process I was invited to join a leadership training seminar that dramatically changed my management style and ultimately aided the planning process. The seminar was organized by Synectics, a business firm in Cambridge, MA. Synectics offers a creative problem solving approach that builds on participants' ideas so that by the time a solution is reached, everyone has contributed and has a stake in it (Mohl, 1986). I immediately utilized the newly acquired philosophy and problem solving techniques by involving staff in "brainstorming" department structures, both short- and long-term. We prioritized our guiding principles, roles and responsibilities. We actively surveyed other hospitals and drew schemas of various structural combinations. I became much more active both in leading the restructure meetings and formulating new ideas based on full staff input. A new structure seemed to evolve out of the drawings that all staff participated in.

Of special note and implicit in our new organizational chart is a matrix organization, with dual accountability relationships within the organizational structure (Allcorn, 1990). In place of a traditional top-down management, we have instituted the interlocking of traditional clinical accountability with program accountability. This system calls upon individual as well as collective staff accountability to achieve the Department goals of counseling patients and families, discharge planning, and continuing care. Within several months we will begin to evaluate our new structure and determine if it best meets patient care and staff needs.

REFLECTIONS ON SOCIAL WORK MANAGEMENT

As I look around at Social Work Department Director colleagues, it seems that many of us were selected not necessarily because we had demonstrated superb management skills prior to our new jobs, but rather because we were recognized clinicians who were politically savvy or well known within our institutions for being highly responsible. All of these factors are important, yet, certainly in my case, not nearly sufficient to prepare me to manage and lead such a large staff in an academic setting, where not only clinical expertise but scholarship, grantsmanship, and fiscal accountability are essential. Many of these skills I have learned over the past five years. Some, in fact, I may have even mastered. Early on I identified many of my deficits and sought out people within my institution for assistance, i.e., Human Resources and the Budget Office. An outside leadership seminar also provided ideas and inspiration.

For social workers aspiring to management positions, however, I would not recommend this hit-or-miss approach. There needs to be a more formal approach to learning the necessary tools that prepare social workers to be leaders both within our hospitals as well as within the larger arena of health care.

Currently, I am involved with the Simmons College Graduate

School for Health Studies in designing just such a curriculum. As proposed, the Certificate of Advanced Graduate Study in Health Care Administration will specifically prepare clinical social workers whose current responsibilities and/or future goals require health care management skills. Courses such as legal issues in health care, health care policy, managed care, human resources management, ethical issues in administrative decision making, and marketing of social work services will be offered.

Given today's complex health care system, we can no longer simply grow-up in our jobs. This certificate program assumes that we bring the strengths of our work experience to the classroom, and in combination with course work, prepare ourselves for leadership in the challenging field of health care administration.

CONCLUSION

The Beth Israel Hospital, like other hospitals, is currently at a crossroads. Although it continues to maintain patient care as its foundation and teaching and research as the remaining primary mission areas, it is evaluating its delivery of health care in a cost effective manner. Patients are becoming more intense, we are rapidly expanding into specialized, ambulatory service areas, and are increasing the number of intensive care beds. As Director, these changes will affect the Social Work Department and the profession, as they give direction and focus to our future practice. I face the challenge of continuing to be not only innovative in patient care services and program planning, but also flexible in our roles and relationships in order to meet a world where technology and economics evolve faster than we can describe.

REFERENCES

Allcorn, S. (1990). Using matrix organization to manage health care delivery organizations. *Hospital and Health Services Administration*, 35(4), 575-590.
Berger, C., Ph.D. (1991). Downsizing by any other name means cutbacks. *Social Work Administration*, Summer, 8-10.
Beth Israel Hospital (1992, February), Social Work Department. *Mission Statement*. Boston, MA.

Beth Israel Hospital (1989). *PREPARE/21 Plan for the 21st Century*. Boston, MA.

Crampton, K., Werner, D., & Regina, V. (1978). Matrix structure in a large-hospital ambulatory service. *Journal of Ambulatory Case Management*, July, 65-74.

Johnson, R., & Berger, C. (1990). The challenge of change: enhancing social work services at a time of cutback. *Health and Social Work*, 15(3), 181-190.

Mayer, J., et al. (1990). Empowering families of the chronically ill: A partnership experience in a hospital setting. *Social Work in Health Care*, 14, 73-90.

Mohl, B. (1986, January). Unlocking the creative mind. *The Boston Globe*, pp. 46-48.

Moore, T., & Lorimer, B. (1976). The matrix organization in business and health care institutions: A comparison. *Hospital and Health Services Administration*, Fall, 26-34.

Prince, G. (1982). *Group Planning and Problem Solving Methods in Engineering*. New York: John Wiley and Sons, Inc.

Ryan, J. (1980). Better style for change: Matrix management. *Hospitals*, November, 105-108.

Zaleznik, A. (1992). Managers and leaders: Are they different? *Harvard Business Review*, March-April, 126-135.

The Evolution of Social Work
in a Community Hospital

Pamela L. Ruster, ACSW

INTRODUCTION

Reflecting on twelve years as a social work administrator has provided a unique time to consider important career markings. The people who contributed to the position of strength and respect for social work are the same individuals who provided challenge and an environment for social work to flourish. The accomplishment of developing a social work department from the early stages to a mature department with high credibility within the hospital facility was something I took for granted and success was the expected outcome. At times when success was not achievable within the hospital system, energy was placed externally. When opportunity returned for internal success the social work department thrived and developed along with the larger hospital system.

My reflections have taken me beyond the obvious considerations of department growth and development. Organizational power issues facing the profession will be addressed including obtaining, maintaining and regaining institutional support.

There are four key events which impacted the department's integration within the larger hospital. They include:

Pamela L. Ruster is Director of Social Work, Indiana University Medical Center, 550 North University Boulevard, Indianapolis, IN 46202-5250.

[Haworth co-indexing entry note]: "The Evolution of Social Work in a Community Hospital." Ruster, Pamela L. Co-published simultaneously in *Social Work in Health Care* (The Haworth Press, Inc.) Vol. 20, No. 4, 1995, pp. 73-88; and: *Social Work Leadership in Healthcare: Directors' Perspectives* (ed: Gary Rosenberg, and Andrew Weissman), The Haworth Press, Inc., 1995, pp. 73-88. Multiple copies of this article/chapter may be purchased from The Haworth Document Delivery Center [1-800-3-HAWORTH; 9:00 a.m. - 5:00 p.m. (EST)].

- Physician support
- Family Practice and Obstetric Referral Program
- Rehabilitation services
- Quality Improvement Process

These events will be discussed within the framework of the history of the department and the other factors affecting hospital culture. Collaborative practice will be delineated while describing various stages of department growth.

HISTORICAL PERSPECTIVE

Columbus Regional Hospital (known as Bartholomew County Hospital until 1992) is a 325 acute care hospital founded in the early 1900's. Bartholomew County is a rural community 45 miles south of Indianapolis and has a total population of 70,000 people. Columbus is an affluent community of 36,000 known for the highest per capita income in the state of Indiana. Columbus is home to two Fortune 400 companies and has been the recipient of numerous endowments for architectural excellence. Hospital services include specialty programs in psychiatry, cancer services and rehabilitation. The geographic service area consists of twelve counties in southeastern Indiana.

My medical social work experiences began here in January 1980. A former colleague had just assumed the post of manager of the social services department: the first MSSW to be hired. Following one field placement, a master's thesis, and a four month part time position I accepted a full time position as a medical social worker in February 1981, one month following MSSW graduation.

The social services department consisted of a secretary, manager, one MSW and one BSW in the position of a patient representative. In August, 1981 I was offered the manager position, and I was faced with sorting through complex factors to make a decision. The competing factors were centered on my desire to learn and have a mentor, to be a strong and productive department member, and to be a generalist, providing social work services in a rural, progressive, one hospital community. I recognized that I was in the right place at either the right time or the wrong time, depending on how I interpreted the opportunity. I opted for the right time scenario.

The hospital management structure of the early days and that of the current administration vaguely resemble one another. The power base was simple: nursing ruled, and the loudest were the most powerful. In 1976 the Social Services department was created due to JCAHO regulations that mandated the provision of social work to meet the needs of inpatients. The department consisted of one non-social worker who facilitated resources to meet concrete demands. In May, 1979 the first MSSW was hired, and the quest for professional definition began. Social work did not flourish under this administration. The evolution was slow and not without setbacks and lean years.

At the time of my field placement in January 1980 only physicians or nurses who had experienced social work while in residency programs or other training had knowledge of social work. No systems existed for further integration or collaborative practice. Nursing consisted predominantly of diploma nurses and provided all discharge planning. One nursing supervisor was designated as the coordinator for all nursing home placements. Social work initially reported to the medical records department, later it reported to a nurse with responsibilities for professional services.

The first break through for social work occurred with the creation of the hospital's first multidisciplinary team. A neurologist was interested in obtaining patient information in an organized manner. A four bed nursing unit was designated for stroke patients. Under his auspices, social work, physical therapy, occupational therapy and speech therapy joined with nursing to improve services to persons with a stroke diagnosis. This team marked the beginning recognition of social work within the context of the larger organization.

Historically, the team concept of collaboration gained recognition during the post World War II era in the 1950's with a concern to provide for disabled veterans (Germain, 1984). The recognition that contributions can be made by several disciplines working together eventually became evident in Columbus. Patients benefited from coordination of services, social work began receiving referrals for a multitude of patient problems. Neurology began including social work consultation for the majority of inpatients. Much latitude was given for social work to provide therapeutic interventions along with the discharge planning core services. Opportunities developed for communication with other colleagues and physician groups. Social work often was discovered by other physicians while seeing patients along with the neurology staff.

Schoenberg (1975) discusses the impact of the roles of collaboration and the formative processes which must occur. The impact that social work would have within the organization was not realized for many years, yet the retrospective review of the development of the collaborative process is intriguing when placed within the context of Schoenberg's (1975) model. Schoenberg presents five progressive stages of collaboration: (1) Role separation; (2) Overestimation and disappointment; (3) Realistic Appraisal; (4) Accommodation and (5) Integration of roles (Germain 1984, Schoenberg 1975).

In the early years of development the role separation model is portrayed. Disciplines politely acknowledged the other, with little understanding or appreciation for the uniqueness of the other. Eventually social work became viewed as an integrated program which demonstrated leadership across administrative lines. It took a long time and was conflict ridden. Social work was perceived by some administration members as threatening, possibly due to our advanced education. The only other master's prepared employees were speech pathologists and audiologists. Additionally, social work advocated for patients and their families. As a department we began to question long standing practices which infringed upon patient rights or privacy issues. As nursing began to struggle with professional identity issues and more opportunity was available for baccalaureate nurses, nursing administration appeared to strengthen the resolve that nursing was self-sufficient and could exist in isolation.

During this time, Schoenberg's second stage was reached, overestimation and disappointment. Without nursing's desire to collaboratively develop new relationships within the organization, our ability to forge ahead independently was thwarted. The therapy departments were segregated and no format existed for cooperative projects or networking outside of rehabilitation team meetings. We were able to increase staffing in limited areas; however, in 1984 through attrition we lost one position. Eventually this era (1985-89) gave way to a resurgence of growth in social work. New opportunities became possible when new reporting responsibilities were assigned as new administrative staff were added. Hospital leadership changed and a previously strong nursing advocate with a thirty year history with the organization left. An opportunity once again for social work to establish collaborative relationships through which credibility could be established emerged.

In the third stage, realistic appraisal, opportunities for hospital program development began. With this came blurring of professional boundaries as each discipline became more aware of how others could contribute to shared goals. This was demonstrated through shared leadership and planning opportunities. Accommodation, the fourth stage of collaboration, became evident. Disciplines became complimentary in their roles. An example of a program which evolved from a single focus to integrated care is a three county obstetric referral program developed in 1980 at the request of the Department of Obstetrics to decrease or eliminate the number of women presenting for delivery who had received no prenatal care. Low income women are assigned a physician who received a copy of our psychosocial assessment. The patient received in depth case management services. In 1991 the fifth stage of collaboration evolved to reflect an interdisciplinary program including dietitians and home care nursing. Social work has been formally recognized in the counties served as the coordinator of all case management services.

Currently, social work reports to a division director, under the auspices of the Chief Operating Officer of the hospital. The hospital corporation is but one of the businesses including an ambulance company, durable medical equipment company, home health care, hospice and the area mental health agency. Social work is grouped with the rehabilitation therapies: occupational, physical and speech/audiology. Reporting to this section in the hospital has been instrumental in the position of influence. The revenue base to which we belong became crucial as rehabilitation became the most profitable medical specialty in the hospital. Virtually all program growth and departmental expansion was within this division. During this same time, accountability for the chaplain and volunteer community clergy programs were added to the responsibilities of the social work manager.

DEPARTMENT FUNCTIONS AND PROGRAMS

The social work department scope of services includes discharge planning, crisis intervention, information and referral, counseling and consultation and community case management services. Working jointly with nurse discharge planners, patients are screened for complex discharge planning needs. Nurse discharge planners provide for nursing home transfers and home care needs for the medical/surgical population 65 and older. Social work provides advocacy services and counseling to patients/families and significant others for identified dilemmas or conflict regarding nursing home placement decisions. Social work is the primary provider for all patients under age 65, and coordinates abuse and neglect cases (adult and child). Nurse discharge planning staff are under the direction of the utilization management department and have performed their current duties since the 1970's.

Other primary areas for social work include the psychiatric program, DRG exempt 24 bed rehabilitation unit, cardiology services and cancer center services. In all of the above mentioned programs, social work is defined as case manager.

A program closely related to the previously mentioned obstetric program is the physician medicaid referral program. In 1976 when social services first began, the Department of Family Practice requested a system to assign medicaid families or individuals a family practice physician. Social work has become the county medicaid gate keeper. Besides assigning the counties' 2% medicaid population a physician, as physicians relocate, retire, or die, patients are re-assigned to other physicians. This has been an opportunity for high visibility within Family Practice; however, it has also been a source of much turmoil as physician practices have capped the number of medicaid recipients they perceive to be their "fair share." At one point in 1990 only one physician was accepting new medicaid patients, eventually he closed his practice and relocated. An opportunity presented for negotiation with the department of Family Practice and re-commitment was achieved from 100% of the physician groups. Physicians and administration looked to social work for direction to regain a balance. Our role was not only that of negotiator, but also that of community conscience and responsibility.

In 1983 social work was approached by a physician to begin

office based outpatient mental health services. Services were to be of a limited nature, and would provide for continuity of patient care. No other community service existed which would meet the medical social work needs of these patients. A proposal was submitted to hospital administration and they refused. The hospital was not philosophically committed to outpatient practice nor did they support the concept of providing services outside hospital walls. Basic concerns regarding conflict of interest as well as questions regarding loyalty to the hospital organization were raised. Department members entered into a contract privately with the physician to provide the services during off hours. These services continued for three years, until a change in hospital administration occurred. A new President was hired and gradually expanded the definition of the hospital scope of services.

To remain interested in the same position over a number of years I knew that I would need to be in an environment where creativity and enthusiasm for change was evident. As the climate of the organization changed, more opportunities emerged for social work to diversify. The organization began to take on more characteristics which would reward those behaviors. Also, the goals of the organization became enmeshed with community responsibility. Hospital administration had demonstrated an attitude of separateness from the community in the early 80's. The new administration shifted focus and began to understand that the hospital needed the community support in order to successfully compete in an expanding market place which now extended 50 miles north to Indianapolis.

After several years of discussion, in 1991 social work fee for service was initiated for inpatients and outpatients. Prior to that time revenues had been received on a limited basis for various activities. These included social work consultations to area nursing homes, an emergency response program and stress management educational programs. Also, the physician office based outpatient program was eventually embraced by the hospital as low risk and income received was transferred to a hospital account. Recognizing the tenuous fiscal situation towards which health care was headed, the mission to achieve fee for service continued to be a department goal. The staff were slow to assimilate the information and develop enthusiasm for the program. Over time we had an opportunity to educate, discuss, and debate over the value conflicts that initiating charges seems to bring for staff. In late 1990 a new vice president for finance was added to the management team and the issue was re-initiated. A successful outcome was attributed to strong administrative and medical support, as well as clear expectations from the finance office.

MANAGEMENT STYLE

During sixteen years, the department grew from three individuals to thirteen. The structure of a department is closely related to how decisions are made and supported (Lewis, 1983).

A participative group model is a management style that reflects the confidence that leaders have in the group, a constancy of purpose, thorough communication across the organization, and motivation based on responsibility and participation. This system is noted for worker autonomy and commitment to a common organizational goal (Likert, 1967, Germain, 1984).

This model most closely fits the Columbus Regional Hospital Structure. Individuals within the department maintained responsibility for their actions and the workings of the department.

Conflict between individual professional concerns and loyalty to the agency goals can be lessened through active participation by staff in setting priorities (Lewis, 1979). As the department grew, staff participation in decision making was an accepted way of doing business. The social workers were encouraged to represent themselves on committees and in planning for their specific areas of practice. Individual staff members were responsible for establishing both a knowledge base and personal relationships within their practice area. Staff developed unique and creative methods for integration into specific areas of practice. The department was developed on the management perspective that utilization of employee's potential was a direct correlation to their ability to integrate themselves.

The director has the responsibility of preparing department members to manage the department in the director's absence. Individuals are selected and mentored to assume this role. This can only be accomplished if clear lines of responsibility are drawn, and all players understand and accept their role in the larger organizational structure. We have two levels of work to do: the work of the patient, and the work of the department. The work of the patient is the ongoing case consultation and assessment on behalf of the patients and their families or significant others. The work of the department is the ongoing education, professional growth and development, community relations, management of information and regulatory standards.

Two staff meetings are conducted monthly. The first is for the work of the department to be conducted. The second is organized by the staff inservice coordinator based on educational programs the staff have attended. The staff are required to provide two per year to their peers. The educational inservice coordinator is an assigned role, with no remuneration and is rotated among staff.

KNOWLEDGE AND SKILLS

Skills are developed both out of necessity, and planned strategy. Practice, trial and error, and increased self awareness are all methods by which we build a repertoire of skills. The major areas are:

- Networking: Collaboration on projects that share common goals and purpose form lasting relationships
- Maintain a focus: choose battles to win the war, not the skirmish
- Problem solving: being a part of solutions, not just identifying problems.
- Financial management: budgeting as well as development of a solid financial bottom line
- Evaluation skills: learning to evaluate staff work performance and provide positive feedback along with areas for growth
- Team work in a host setting; sounds easier than it really is
- Gaining administration's respect for a macro or global perspective of the organization
- Demonstrating what we can do that no one else can: finding our organizational niche

QUALITY INITIATIVE

Social work took an early role in the quality initiative program. In 1990 the hospital committed to quality, and the new quality coach came from an environment where social work was a part of the process. Social work has a strong affinity with quality management philosophy. As Kiltman (1979) points cut, "More often than not . . . individuals assume that their view of the world defines the essence of the problem ." Social work has learned to start where the perception of the problem is. The first individuals who were selected to initiate the facilitator role within the organization represented attributes such as systems thinking, large employee responsibility, and overall acceptance as a leader within the organization. As social work manager I was included. After receiving extensive quality training, our group of five designed the roles and responsibilities for the organization. Subsequently, a member of the social work staff was selected to the facilitator role.

ORIENTATION, EDUCATION AND SUPERVISION

New staff are oriented to the department and the community for approximately two weeks prior to assuming a case load. During that time there are scheduled appointments with department members to provide information regarding the work of the department, legal regulations, documentation formats, and other department specific information. The new staff are also scheduled to meet with individuals in departments with whom they will be regularly interfacing. Community agency interviews are arranged and may continue over the first six months of employment. Key hospital personnel have been identified and they are listed in the departmental policy manual. All new employees, students and volunteers are expected to review the orientation policy, meet the expectations, sign and date the completion.

Supervision is provided for new staff by the department manager. Specific problem solving and case consultation is also provided by the manager. Other informal structures are in place for consultation by peers either by areas of practice or through the development of personal relationships. With decentralization of departmental offices separate offices with one to three staff were created, and sub-groups began to form. Staff decision making groups became a format for case consultation, collaboration and continuity. As the department grew and the chaplaincy program was added, definition of roles became important. A staff member is designated in charge in the absence of the manager, and paid a salary differential if the responsibility extends to five working days or more. At first the role was rotated among all ACSW social work staff who had been on staff for a minimum of one year. Eventually, one staff member expressed an interest in ongoing management opportunities, and officially became the designated individual.

A hospital policy had existed which provided annually $1000 tuition for any employee to enroll in further education through a university program. Departments with entry level requirements such as social work were unable to utilize that benefit. Following discussions with Human Resources, a budget line was proposed which would build the monies directly in social work budget, rather than through Human Resources. Each staff has $1000 per year for education outside of the institution. In the future this may become an area for fiscal restraint. Due to our rural area and status of being the largest hospital for fifty miles, we seek educational opportunities elsewhere. The opportunity for staff to gain information through linkages and contacts with individuals in other parts of the country has supported creativity and energy among staff.

A Performance Appraisal was developed by social work staff that established standards for education that each staff will provide for the department, hospital or community. Additionally all staff are encouraged to participate in professional activities, either NASW, or an organization specific to their area of practice. Staff consciously make a decision concerning their degree of involvement. Dues for NASW are paid annually for staff after achieving ACSW. This was initiated several years prior to 1992 when Indiana's certification regulation went into effect. Third party payor's expected that home care be performed by ACSW's. All staff were involved in home visits for their area of expertise, thus ACSW was an expected practice achievement supported by the department and the hospital.

Social work education of students has played an important role in the history of the department. During years of growth, students who were successful in their placements and fit the timing of staff expansion were successfully hired, thus integrating smoothly into the department culture. We have had students from six baccalaureate and master's programs, with as many as three students at once. Field instructor and task instructor roles exist for qualified staff. Our goal is for students to gain expertise in social work skills and knowledge, rather than becoming skilled with one medical population.

STRATEGIES AND PLANNING OPPORTUNITIES

Each year the department is involved in a yearly planning process. Staff members develop personal and program goals, from which departmental goals with timeframes are established. Additionally three year planning is completed which incorporates projected growth in program areas, trends in caseloads or populations served and additional staffing needs. These are combined with division trends and submitted to the chief operating officer.

Within the Physical Medicine and Rehabilitation Program of the hospital, the social work department was instrumental in the development of the Program Evaluation System (PES) required per the Commission on Accreditation for Rehabilitation Facilities (CARF). In 1988 social work developed a computerized management information system. Our data base supported the sub-categories necessary to create the PES. This enhanced the department's link to the therapies through information and visibly furthered the organizational goal to obtain CARF accreditation. In many organizations the responsibility for meeting the demands of CARF accreditation stays in the areas of the rehabilitation therapies: physical therapy, occupational therapy, and speech. Social work in this case provided the case management role to assist in focusing the team on the common purpose and provided the mechanism for data analysis. No other department had the capability for data collection and analysis. Through team linkages and collaboration we were able to contribute to the larger goal. Although the Annual PES Report is the only research that has been conducted in the department, it is shared internally throughout the organization and has been utilized extensively by the governing body, administration, marketing and medical staff.

COLLABORATIVE NETWORKS

The natural grouping within the rehabilitative therapies became the base for social work. The late 1980's and early 1990's provided a lucrative framework for financial growth in this area. The outpatient therapies were growing in dramatic measure, demanding the attention of hospital administration for added space and additional staff resources. The rehabilitation areas contained natural growth for the social work department as a holistic view of the patient and family evolved, thus adequate staffing was achieved in the rehabilitative programs. A strong team definition emerged as the managers of the rehabilitation departments worked jointly on the CARF accreditation expectations, and after that, maintained the standards we had achieved. We were a well organized team, " . . . characterized by deadlines, work loads, the need for predictable output and the need to make decisions and establish priorities" (Germain 1984, pp. 216, 217).

At the same time, administration in the hospital was changing, with new players joining the management team. As discussed earlier, the chief financial officer was added along with a vice president for human resources. We had an opportunity to become instrumental in (1) lines of supply, (2) lines of information and (3) lines of support. The barriers which had barred the realization of goals such as establishing fee for service for specific inpatient and outpatient services were removed. Social work became revenue producing and our once non-lucrative service was no longer viewed as a drain on resources. Even though we were not recovering all expenses, we were perceived as contributing to the healthy bottom line of the organization.

Staff were successful in creating strong allies in nursing areas. As social work staff numbers grew, a strong identity began to develop. The department took on a higher profile due to numbers, as well as the development of a departmental culture. Professionalism was high, and the approachability by employees for personal counseling issues increased. Even though the hospital corporation maintained an employee assistance program, our informal networking continued to grow. Social work began to relieve nursing staff of crisis management and other patient coordinating responsibilities added to their already burdened staffing ratio.

Department physician advocates vocally supported the work we were accomplishing. Neurology, heading the rehabilitation program, was the strongest proponent, along with the family practice area, psychiatry, pediatrics, obstetrics, and cardiology. As staff were able to define their areas of expertise, produce successful results, and build trust, we were able to grow in the medical specialty areas.

Administratively, credibility was greatly enhanced with the evolution of the quality initiative program. This was achieved through strong involvement in the facilitator program, consultation and relief back up for the quality coach. Additionally, facilitation of the hospital budget team gave way to networking and frequent interaction with both the Vice President of Finance and President.

The majority of networking activities came as a result of collaborative projects. Working in a rural area, many staff come from various neighboring counties involving long distance commutes. All contact with colleagues are made during working hours. Jointly working on projects most efficiently established relationships among peers. Common projects led to common goals which created the depth and professional respect necessary to survive the pressures of the environment.

COMMUNITY INVOLVEMENT

Social work departments and health care agencies serve as links to community support systems. We are at the forefront for knowledge of service gaps, trends in delivery of service as well as customer knowledge. Community linkages can be enhanced by the organizing energy provided by social workers activating a coalition to problem solve shared issues.

Community involvement by staff is encouraged. Time is given from their work load to participate on boards or other community agendas. We have vast state board representation ranging from adolescent pregnancy, NASW, and to national boards representing social work as a profession. Through the years my involvement has included the local child abuse advisory board, health care and referral clinic advisory board, committee chair of the state NASW certification efforts, as well as state and national continuity of care organizations. Some of the activities served as an opportunity for creativity and success when involvement in the hospital system was limited or blocked. Although unaware of that phenomena at the time, I have since labeled it as such.

The environment of Columbus Regional Hospital has been generous by allowing staff time to participate on boards and committees at local, regional and national levels. Through various affiliations our department members have benefited by increased systems and issues knowledge. The professional satisfaction from involvement in external concerns reaps benefits for the organization through community linkages and strengthening of collegial ties. Establishing successful state linkages resulted in the procurement of grant funding for rehabilitation programs and pre-natal programs. As well, community case management brought services together to creatively provide for patients when existing delivery systems were non-existent.

SUMMARY

Since 1905 social work has had the privilege of working with great medical leaders who have respected and assisted our profession. As predicted in 1984 by Abraham Lurie,

> The social work department of the future will be more decentralized . . . develop stronger links administratively . . . knowledge of changing social problems . . . legislation, research, computerization, data gathering and retrieval.

The Columbus Regional Hospital Social Work department is still early in its development, yet the above predictors have occurred which strengthened social work role and professional practice.

By 1992 the following areas served as a strong foundation for the department's continued growth:

- Resource acquisition
- Hospital Integration
- Physician Support

We must continue to advocate for improved care along with providing an environment of compassion for the patients and their families who seek services. Through continued participation on hospital committees such as ethics, and utilization review, we can demonstrate our practice and influence the environment. By creatively accessing resources we can influence and shape opportunities for colleagues. As a social work manager I thank those who have come before me who laid framework, fought battles and defined territory. We need to continue to support one another through collaborative processes and shared experiential learnings.

REFERENCES

Commission on Accreditation for Rehabilitation Facilities. (1992). Standards for Accreditation.

Falck, Hans S. (1990). "Observations on the Scientific Base of Health Social Work." Social Work in Health Care, 15:1.

Germain, Carel B. (1984). Social Work Practice in Health Care. New York: Free Press.

Gerth, H.H. & Mills, C.W. (Eds.). (1958). From Max Weber: Essays in Sociology. New York: Oxford University Press.

Katz, D. & Kahn, R.L. (1978). The Social Psychology of Organizations. Second Ed. New York: John Wiley & Sons.

Kiltmann, K.H. (1978). Problem Management: A Behavioral Science Approach. In G. Zaltman (Ed.), Management Principles for non-profit agencies and organizations. New York: AMACOM.

Lewis, J. & Lewis, M. (1977). Community Counseling: A human services approach. New York: Wiley.

Lewis, J. & Lewis, M. (1983). Management of Human Service Programs. Belmont, CA: Wadsworth Press.

Likert, R. (1961). New Patterns of Management. New York: McGraw-Hill.

Likert, R. (1967). The Human Organization: It's Management and Value. New York: McGraw-Hill.

Lurie, Abraham. (1984). "Social Work in Health Care in the Next Ten Years." Social Work Administration in Health Care. New York: The Haworth Press, Inc.

Lurie, Abraham. (1992). "Through the Looking Glass: A 40 Year Retrospective." Social Work in Health Care, 16:3, 5-11.

Marcus, L.J. (1990). "Research on Organizational Issues in Health Care Social Work." Social Work in Health Care, 15:1, 79-95.

Schoenberg, B. (1975). "Interdisciplinary Education: Role Strain and Adaptations," Seminar Reports, No. 2, New York: Columbia University.

Effective Leadership:
The Healthcare Social Work Director

William J. Spitzer, PhD, ACSW

ORGANIZATIONAL BACKGROUND/RESPONSIBILITIES

For six and a half years between 1986 and 1992, my role was that of Director of Social Work Services at Oregon Health Sciences University (OHSU) in Portland Oregon. As the largest medical facility and only health care university in Oregon, OHSU is one of the pre-eminent patient care, medical research and education centers in the Pacific Northwest.

Licensed for 500+ beds, OHSU includes University Hospital, Doernbecher Children's Hospital, schools of medicine, nursing and dentistry, the Child Development and Rehabilitation Center, Center for Health Care Ethics, Vollum Institute for Advanced Biomedical Research, Casey Eye Center, Center for Rural Health Care and more than fifty outpatient clinics offering both primary and specialty care. It functions as one of only two Level 1 Emergency Trauma Centers in Oregon and maintains the state's Emergency Services Communication Center. With an annual budget of approximately $300 million, OHSU is Oregon's eighth, and Portland's fourth, largest employer with over 7,000 faculty and staff.

William J. Spitzer is Director of Social Work Services at the Medical College of Virginia and Clinical Associate Professor, School of Social Work at Virginia Commonwealth University.

[Haworth co-indexing entry note]: "Effective Leadership: The Healthcare Social Work Director." Spitzer, William J. Co-published simultaneously in *Social Work in Health Care* (The Haworth Press, Inc.) Vol. 20, No. 4, 1995, pp. 89-109; and: *Social Work Leadership in Healthcare: Directors' Perspectives* (ed: Gary Rosenberg, and Andrew Weissman), The Haworth Press, Inc., 1995, pp. 89-109. Multiple copies of this article/chapter may be purchased from The Haworth Document Delivery Center [1-800-3-HAWORTH; 9:00 a.m. - 5:00 p.m. (EST)].

While the medical school dates to 1887, it was not until 1974 that the merger of the medical, dental and nursing schools with the hospitals and clinics led to the creation of the University of Oregon Health Sciences Center as a separate institution under the direction of the Oregon State System of Higher Education. The institution was renamed the Oregon Health Sciences University in 1981. The preponderance of OHSU patients are derived from the three counties comprising the greater Portland area of 1.5 million. At the time, the facility maintained an 85% occupancy rate and was one of the largest providers of indigent care in the state.

As Director, I held ultimate responsibility for the planning, budgeting, implementation and monitoring of social work services throughout the facility. This included activities in the in- and outpatient, adult and pediatric areas, as well as administration of the facility's Financial Assistance Specialist Program, which is responsible for screening and opening Medicaid cases among in- and outpatients.

In addition to these duties, I served in numerous capacities within OHSU extending beyond the social work department. My long-term interest in staff development and training led to involvement and, ultimately, Chairmanship of the OHSU Education and Training Committee. As Chair of the OHSU Patient Emphasis Task Force, I facilitated development of a program proposal emphasizing patient and family care through collaboration of employee teams located throughout the university hospitals and outpatient clinics.

Concern about insuring readily available emotional support to facility staff experiencing critical incident stress associated with patient care led to a leadership role in developing the OHSU Stress Debriefing Team and responsibility as Project Coordinator. Previous child welfare experience contributed to my collaboration with the Director of the Rosenfeld Center for the Study of Child Abuse and Neglect regarding the OHSU Suspected Child Abuse and Neglect (SCAN) Team and Primary Investigator status on a grant proposal to create a large scale child abuse intervention and education program. Other professional interests and experience prompted my participation in the facility's Disaster Planning Committee, Trauma Operations Forum, Advance Directives Task Force, and Management Forum.

External professional activities were a significant component of my position and encouraged by hospital administration as evidence of facility leadership in the community. Reflecting my particular interest in social work education, I maintained an adjunct faculty appointment as Assistant Professor of Social Work at Portland State University with responsibilities including development and teaching of the health care policy course, curriculum consultation, internship program development and student supervision. Upon moving to Virginia, my educational involvement continued with acceptance of an appointment at Virginia Commonwealth University School of Social Work, designation as Site Accreditation Reviewer for the Council on Social Work Education, appointment as a Contributing Editor to *Health and Social Work* and publication authorship.

Interest in overall professional practice led to membership on the NASW Oregon Chapter Board of Directors, the NASW Advisory Board to the State Clinical Social Work Licensing Board and the NASW Minority Student Scholarship Committee. During my five year tenure as first State Continuing Education Chair for NASW, I had the opportunity to design, implement and maintain a statewide program that certified over 500 formal educational offerings and issued nearly 19,000 continuing education certificates to conference attendees.

Within the realm of community services, I served for four years as the first State Clinical Director of the 100 member Oregon Critical Response Team (OCRT). This included a leadership role in OCRT's 1989 evolution as one of the few statewide critical stress debriefing teams in the United States designed to support emergency first-responder personnel following traumatic interventions.

Because of its immediate relevance to my department directorships, my most active involvement and identification was, and continues to be, with the Society for Social Work Administrators in Health Care. The personal and professional friendships derived from this association are among the most meaningful I have known, proving invaluable to me over the years as a source of encouragement and wisdom. In return, during my OHSU tenure I had the opportunity to offer assistance to the Oregon Society as a two-term President, five year State Board Member and Chair of the Education Committee that developed Oregon's first statewide social work health care practice conference. In my five year tenure as the State Society's first Chair of the Graduate Education Committee, our Society enhanced its relationships with the School of Social Work, influenced the expansion of health care curriculum offerings and established a formal recognition award jointly conferred by the Oregon Society and Portland State University to MSW candidates specializing in health care practice (Spitzer, 1990).

My involvement with the Society preceded my move to Oregon and continues with my relocation to Virginia. As a department director in Illinois, I participated with the Illinois Board of Directors, functioned as Editor and Publisher of the State Newsletter and as Vice-President of the Central Illinois Chapter. At the national level, it was my honor to be appointed as a member, and then ultimately Chair, of the Hy Weiner Leadership Award Committee and to serve for four years on the Education for Practice in Health Care Committee. Since moving to Virginia, I have been appointed to the National SSWAHC/AHA Political Action Steering Committee and function on the State Society Board.

ENTRY INTO THE POSITION

My involvement in health and health care delivery began during my social work graduate studies at the University of Illinois at Urbana/Champaign. During that time I developed a private practice employing five MSW's to provide patient care and program consultation to skilled and intermediate care nursing facilities in Illinois and Indiana. While these activities were divergent from my earlier MSW focus on children and family services, I found them engaging from both a clinical and organizational standpoint-factors that ultimately prompted my career selection of healthcare practice

After receiving a PhD in social work with a business administration concentration, I assumed a number of management capacities over a four and a half year tenure at Sarah Bush Lincoln Health System in east-central Illinois. Although my primary function was to serve as Director of Social Work, one year prior to my appointment in Oregon I additionally assumed administrative oversight of the Health System's Department of Human Resources and the Midwest Professional Registry, a for-profit subsidiary providing home health care. Other social work duties at the time included developing and managing a Social Work consultation program for long term care facilities that was modeled on my private practice. Additionally, as Chairperson, I contributed to establishing the county's Suspected Child Abuse/Neglect (SCAN) Team, served as Vice-President of the county Interagency Coordination Council and continued to develop my private consulting practice. Because of other professional commitments, my private practice activities evolved to administration of an expanding MSW staff rather than provision of direct service.

The principal attraction of OHSU was the opportunity to pursue my management interests and the practice of social work in a larger setting, with a shift from a community hospital to an urban, academic, tertiary care institution. Particularly appealing were OHSU's scope of service, desires for program development and staff enhancement, the additional prospect of serving as faculty with the only CSWE graduate social work school in Oregon and potentially functioning in statewide leadership roles. My fundamental focus was on moving the department to the forefront of patient care, education and research, not just within the institution, but on a regional and national level.

The transition to OHSU also provided occasion to function in a complex management matrix of division, department, program, clinic and special service directors. The university is comprised of two major components—the academic schools and programs and the hospitals and clinics. The latter are the responsibility of the Hospital Director who, like the academic deans in the various schools, reports to the University President. Within the hospital and clinic system, Associate Directors provide leadership to nursing, professional services, fiscal services, facility planning, ambulatory care/centers of excellence and physical plant/support services.

My initial reporting relationship as Director of Social Work Services was to the Associate Hospital Director for Planning. Hospital administration, however, experienced significant changes in personnel and function during my tenure. The implication of these changes was to shift accountability for Social Work five times, from Planning to Fiscal Services, back to Planning, then to an Acting Associate Director, Acting Assistant Director and ultimately to a newly appointed, permanent Associate Director of Professional Services. These numerous and seemingly discontinuous changes proved valuable in advancing the department in both the short and long term by affording the opportunity to familiarize a number of administrative personnel with the characteristics, functions and potentialities of contemporary health care social work practice.

While each new administrator expressed interest in the applications of social work to patient care operations, the scope of their knowledge about the profession and department services often meant that social work planning proposals were accompanied by indepth discussions regarding each idea's short and long term merit. The ongoing dialogue with the administrators, coupled with their understanding and commitment, enabled the Department to develop both the scope and sophistication of social work practice within the institution. Concomitant with its broadened patient care responsibilities and service areas, the department expanded over a six year period by approximately sixteen staff to 34.5 FTEs in 42 positions, consisting of MSW, Bachelors and secretarial support staff. Service expansion occurred in ambulatory care, liver, cardiac and renal transplantation, oncology, neurology, trauma and pediatric areas, with additional provisions for a Department Supervisor, "utility" or float staff, secretarial support and a new five member Financial Specialist Group.

DEPARTMENT PROFILE AND MANAGEMENT STRUCTURE

At the time, OHSU hospital and clinic social workers were budgeted, recruited, supervised and evaluated through the department. There was a clearly stated expectation from the social work department, however, that its staff maintain an identity with the service areas in which they functioned. This intentionally underscored the multi-disciplinary team nature of patient care delivery and the evolving focus on program or "service line" operations in the facility. For staff, such expectations were met through their consultation in individual patient care and program operations, as well as ongoing participation in unit activities such as team meetings, inservices and planning sessions. Evaluative input from hospital staff assisted probationary and ongoing social work performance evaluations by identifying the extent and nature of the individual contribution to patients, families and program staff.

Functions of the social work department during my tenure were diversified and complex, extending beyond the hospital and clinics to the outside community. Primary department responsibilities were associated with direct patient care, particularly the characteristic discharge planning activities of assessment, consultation, supportive counseling, advocacy, crisis intervention, information/referral and resource arrangement. Expectations for social work engagement with in- and outpatients were high, with approximately 40% of all admissions receiving some form of social work intervention.

In addition to direct patient care, social work services included extensive ongoing education to medical and allied health personnel regarding psychosocial dimensions of health and health care, resource acquisition and social work practice, assistance with facility employee counseling and stress debriefing services. Staff had board or consultative roles in community agencies, administrative and clinical leadership of the Oregon Statewide Critical Response Team (OCRT), classroom teaching and intern preceptorships with Portland State University Graduate School of Social Work and active involvement with an array of state and national social work organizations. Education, research and community service activities were encouraged as part of the professional social work role in a tertiary health care institution. While the timing and nature of how these activities were pursued by staff varied dependent on individual interests, concurrent duties and personal readiness, an expectation was conveyed through supervision and department meetings that staff respond to, or generate, leadership opportunities transcending direct patient care.

On assuming the directorship, the administrative structure of the department consisted of the Department Director, Administrative Assistant/Secretary and a "Casework Supervisor" responsible for monitoring the activities of three non-MSW "casework" staff. Staff were primarily assigned to inpatient units; outpatient coverage was minimal. Role differentiation was limited between MSW and non-MSW staff and, except for the three caseworkers, there were no organizational provisions within the department reflecting congruent staff assignments or responsibilities.

Subsequent modifications in the department structure served to better focus staff skills while deploying across a broader spectrum of patient care areas. Increased emphasis by the department on ambulatory care and continuity with inpatient units led to new clinic positions, assignment of personnel by service and efforts to have staff assume responsibilities for both in- and outpatient care when feasible. This effort was aided over time by expanding hospital efforts to concentrate patient populations, such as oncology, on particular nursing units. Staff intensified their knowledge of the biopsychosocial patient conditions, specialized resources, care needs and professional expectations associated with their individual service areas. Creation of six department divisions for medical and surgical services, transplantation and dialysis, child and maternal services, psychiatric, emergency department/oncall and clerical support further encouraged resource and practice information sharing in monthly discussions, case reviews and training sessions among personnel with similar interests and responsibilities. Group Leaders, serving in lead worker roles, had responsibilities to facilitate regular meetings, orchestrate coverage, assist in program planning and provide input to the director and supervisor on the individual and collective efforts of the work unit.

In support of multi-level staffing, the pairing of MSWs and non-MSW "Social Service Specialists" into newly created teams within oncology, neurology and renal services encouraged use of the most qualified personnel at the appropriate time. MSW staff concentrated on indepth psychosocial evaluations, psychotherapy, crisis intervention and clinical consultation, while redesignated "Specialists" primarily focused on early identification and response to patient and family resource needs associated with discharge planning. Frequent communication between Specialists and MSWs in these areas aided timely triaging and mutual understanding of case status, needs and disposition.

Overall operational management was furthered with the addition of a Department Supervisor. This experienced individual supplemented my supervision by contributing issue specific consultation with the staff, maintaining oversight on Departmental coverage, assisting in continuous quality improvement and program planning efforts and regularly meeting with the Group Leaders to identify and respond to service issues. Importantly, by completing extensive formal training in health care ethics, the Supervisor was able to provide expertise on complex patient care issues, not only to Department staff, but throughout the facility as a member of the Ethics Consultation Service.

PROFESSIONAL DEVELOPMENT

Provision of ongoing training to department staff and contribution to social work education were regarded as important departmental activities. While these should be characteristic components of any professional social work department, positioning in a tertiary, university affiliated hospital setting further underscored the expectation of their presence in our instance. Involvement in these activities not only benefitted individual staff by broadening their practice related experiences but drew the department closer to the professional community through active participation in conferences, presentations, teaching and other related activities. Gains in the practice competencies of individual staff and visibility of the department by emphasized networking within the community subsequently enhanced our posture as a social work practice leader.

Reorganization of the department provided one set of opportunities to focus on continuing staff education. Each functional group within the department was expected to consider staff development as part of their agenda. The relevance of each educational activity was maximized for the target social work group because each maintained a responsibility for identifying their ongoing educational needs and tailoring an appropriate training response. An additional effect was to significantly increase the total number of department educational offerings available to staff over the course of a year. Attendance was expected for those within the sponsoring group and optional for all other staff. Activities of each group were communicated in the general staff meeting and by posting of a calendar. If the topic was of wide spread relevance to the staff, presentations would be made in the monthly general staff meeting. Issues such as implementation of advance directives policies and use of certain community resources were included in this category.

Educational sessions conducted within the department and facility were augmented by staff attendance at outside conferences. Staff were actively encouraged to participate in regional and national activities associated with their particular fields of practice, increasingly as invited presenters or as organizational leader. Conference brochures and requests for papers were conspicuously posted in the department, with focused discussion in supervision on how conference attendance positively impacted both individual staff career development and the education of other facility staff through subsequent inservices. As Chair of the Oregon NASW Continuing Education Program, I was able to additionally share information about relevant forthcoming conferences and seminars. To maximize conference attendance, negotiations were held whenever possible between staff, myself and my counterpart service area directors regarding ways to split costs among those benefitting from the attending staff member's expanded abilities or knowledge. The importance attached to this issue, coupled with the department's continuing expansion contributed to annual revisions of this line item in the budget.

New staff education began with a day-long formal university and hospital/clinic briefing session sponsored by the personnel department. Beginning staff were then matched by our department with a social work "mentor" in the service area to which they would be assigned. An acclimation period with the mentor allowed for increasing new staff members' understanding of duties, unit or service characteristics, other department personnel, facility policies and procedures and work expectations. The department supervisor, office manager and myself provided an overview of the department, presented administrative issues, addressed questions and interests of the staff member and monitored assimilation into the department. A "New Employee Orientation Committee" including interested department personnel as well as new staff reviewed the orientation experience, provided process recommendations and aided staff socialization. This Committee proved to be quite valuable in modifying the orientation process to be as positive, timely and inclusive as possible. Their input led to the evolution of the mentoring system and revisions in information provided to staff.

Staff were similarly encouraged to advance their own formal education, with eight social work and clerical personnel enrolling in

MSW, MS and PhD programs during a six year period. Arrangements were made to facilitate work schedules and provide coverage during periods of class attendance. Based on their knowledge of our operational scope, staff pursuing MSW degrees elected to complete an internship in the department. They expanded their experiences, practice knowledge and skills through assignment in areas unrelated to previous responsibilities or expertise.

Emphasis on professional education extended beyond department staff to MSW candidates from Oregon's only CSWE approved school–Portland State University (PSU). The unique characteristics of OHSU's patient population, complex array of facility services and caliber of social work department operations made it an attractive opportunity for MSW interns specializing in health care practice. As clinical social work staff were expected to embrace educational activities as a component of their professional responsibilities in a tertiary setting, many actively engaged in social work education through guest lecturing, teaching and internship preceptorships.

To enhance the internship experience, consultation with Portland State University led to new OHSU student placement criteria, department internship program guidelines and student performance expectations. The resulting program featured "rotational" placements with "primary" and "secondary" internship instructors assisting second year MSW students in their progression through multiple patient care areas, while an intern group reviewed organizational, management and clinical practice issues (Spitzer and Nash, 1995). The elements of this program evolved from years of discussions with practice and academic colleagues, personal administrative and clinical experience and recommendations in the literature (Berkman and Carlton, 1985; Bogo and Taylor, 1990; Marshack, Davidson and Mizrahi, 1988; Robinovitch and Nash, 1983; Showers and Cuzzi,1991).

My simultaneous activities as adjunct social work faculty, State President and Graduate Education Committee Chair of the Oregon Society for Social Work Administrators in Health Care, Oregon NASW Continuing Education Program Chair and PSU graduate curriculum committee member afforded ample opportunity to impact social work education and practice both in our department and the professional community. Membership on the Education for Practice in Health Care Committee of the National Society for Social Work Administrators in Health Care further enriched both my global perspective on educational issues and ability to make departmental applications.

PROGRAM DEVELOPMENT–
COLLABORATION AND PLANNING

Program planning and budgeting are priority responsibilities for department directors, representing opportunities for the creative application of social work practice within particular institutional settings. Given the complex, ever-changing and competitive nature of these settings, directors must understand and anticipate both facility wide and work unit specific priorities, agendas and constraints. Directors must be able to identify and promptly act on opportunities by proposing relevant, achievable program proposals predicated on social work values and maximizing the application of our professional skills, knowledge and abilities.

At OHSU, information used for preliminary planning was shared with directors through a number of means and at a variety of levels. "Management Forum" meetings with the Hospital Director and other administrators allowed review of facility-wide patient care and budgetary issues, anticipated macro-level program priorities (such as progress on "Centers of Excellence"), legislative impacts on the university and overall operational expectations of departments. A separate monthly meeting of all department, program and clinic directors served as a means of disseminating even more specific information about departmental activities, allowed response to the Management Forum agendas and offered mutual support among facility middle management. Augmenting these monthly Management Forums and directors' meetings were innumerable task forces, committees and work groups that convened throughout the year on a changing array of facility operational issues. Positive working relationships with services such as oncology, pediatrics, ophthalmology and transplant or departments such as admitting and patient accounts increased the likelihood of their consultation with social work when new patient care services were contemplated.

Frequent meetings with social service agencies offered yet additional opportunities to address patient, family and professional concerns while advancing departmental visibility in the community.

The net effect over time was development of a network of contacts which became important to me both as colleagues and friends. It facilitated decision making by guiding one's thoughts about how to approach issues, where to find technical knowledge, professional support and organizational insight. Because of their impact on social work, my involvement in the facility was more frequent with certain medical directors, patient representative and management personnel particularly in nursing, admissions, patient accounts, fiscal services, rehabilitation services and ambulatory care.

Of particular importance to planning and operations were regularly scheduled sessions with my Associate Hospital Director. These sessions allowed for indepth discussion of social work operations, integration of outside information with the specific interests, priorities and perspectives held by the administrator and myself and formation of a management direction best serving all parties involved. The candor and explicitness of my administrator in these meetings was significant in securing a sense of "real" issues and the viability of program initiatives. It focused my individual and department efforts, while affording the administrator an honest and continuously updated perspective of the world from the standpoint of the social work staff. The absence of such a relationship with my administrator would have severely hampered development of facility and department programs, enhancement of staff and promotion of the social work profession within the organization.

Within the department, communication for planning purposes was promoted through ongoing meetings each month with administrative and clinical staff. A 90 minute administrative review of overall operations was held at the beginning of each week with the Department Supervisor, Financial Specialist Supervisor, Office Manager and myself. Information from the facility-wide Management Forum, administrative supervision and other meetings involving social work administrative staff was discussed in light of present and prospective social work services. Communication continued through monthly sessions held by the Department Supervisor with the Department Group Leaders of the child/maternal, medical/surgical, psych and ER/oncall areas. The Leaders, in turn, each met monthly with their groups for purposes of identifying patient care and professional issues, conducting staff development activities and providing mutual support. The Office Manager performed a similar function with department secretarial personnel. Monthly general staff meetings addressed activities of the departmental groups, individual staff and committees, as well as providing information from management forum, community and administrative meetings.

Importantly, staff members were encouraged to exercise their own creativity and social work practice knowledge through ongoing analysis of service needs and program development in their individual areas of responsibility. The result was a myriad of staff initiated patient care groups, policy and procedure input on advance directives, adoptions, trauma response and child abuse reporting, patient and family informational handouts and educational presentations. These efforts were accompanied with positive acknowledgement to the individual, department and profession. In addition to identifying patient acuities and task prioritizations within each department division, staff assisted in creating a new computer based statistical data collection system measuring patient care problems, social work interventions, individual, community and organizational barriers to care and level of staff satisfaction with rendered services. A high-risk prescreening program for select planned admissions, a reimbursed services program for in- and outpatient assessments and counseling and unprecedented contractual cost-sharing arrangements with physicians for new MSW positions in pediatrics, neurology and oncology were further evidence of joint planning efforts initiated by the department.

COMMUNITY RELATIONSHIPS

Major program initiatives warranted collaboration on a wider scale, often including community as well as facility personnel during planning, implementation and operational stages. Social work departments, because of their global, system oriented perspectives, are well-suited to effectively address issues that span the boundaries of hospital and community (Holosio and Taylor, 1989). In these situations, social work can evaluate psychosocial problems, bring together relevant decision-makers and assist in formulation of system responses capable of meeting patient, family and institutional needs.

An illustration of this dynamic occurred in 1986 when OHSU social work staff denoted the inadequacies of the facility's effort to secure hospital funding from potentially eligible Medicaid recipients (Spitzer and Kuykendall, 1994). "Welfare holds" of newly admitted patients sent to the social work department by the admitting office were not effectively or efficiently responded to by social workers pressed with other immediate patient care needs and lacking technical knowledge or connections within the Medicaid program. With information about the problem and related system anomalies provided by staff, and in conjunction with the Admitting Department, approval was obtained from administration and the State Medicaid agency for creation of a highly skilled five member "Financial Specialist Group" within the social work department. These OHSU social work specialists bridged the admitting department personnel, unit social workers and public assistance staff to expediently identify and actually open Medicaid cases. Within one year, the group achieved a verified 91% eligibility determination accuracy rate and, using direct computer linkups with the state Medicaid office to open cases, secured nearly $2.5 million in previously unrealized revenue. Within five years, approximately 6,000 patients were served through this program, with eligibility determination accuracy reaching 99% in 1991, factors influencing our designation as State Social Work Program of the Year.

On an even larger scale, department visibility in the community led to its program planning involvement in the evolution of the Oregon Critical Response Team (OCRT)–one of a very few *statewide* stress debriefing units designed to address the emotional difficulties of traumatic, life threatening rescues by emergency first responder personnel including paramedics, firefighters and police (Neely and Spitzer, 1993; Spitzer and Neely, 1992). Working with the City of Portland Fire Bureau, local clergy, the largest ambulance company in the state and OHSU Emergency Communications, the social work department assisted in putting into operation a program of nearly 100 volunteers stationed throughout the state. Within a three year period OCRT conducted approximately 125 debriefings and 60 educational sessions to over 1200 individuals in Oregon, Washington and California. Four staff from our department, including two with State Board appointments, served OCRT by providing debriefing assistance as well as program consultation. Selected as 1990 State Social Work Program of the Year by the Oregon Society of Social Work Administrators in Health Care, two department staff were further recognized for their contributions by the National Critical Incident Stress Foundation.

When similar emotional support needs surfaced among OHSU health care staff, the department collaborated with other facility personnel to initiate the OHSU Stress Debriefing Team (Spitzer and Burke, 1993). Based in social work, but additionally using the skills of specially trained nurses and physicians, the multidisciplinary team provided assistance not only to OHSU personnel impacted by traumatic patient care situations, but aided several other hospitals in either a debriefing or consultative capacity. In both the OCRT and OHSU instances, social work demonstrated initiative and collaborative resourcefulness in planning and implementing unique programs meeting critical needs.

The collaborative nature of the department extended to its involvement in patient care research. In heart transplantation, for example, interest of the team social worker regarding issues of depression and reintegration of transplanted patients into the work force led to her research collaboration and a series of presentations and publications with medical and social work colleagues from several medical institutions (Maricle et al., 1989; Paris et al., 1992). Similar collaborative efforts by oncology social work staff with the local chapter of the American Cancer Society and Portland State University Graduate School of Social Work influenced selection of the department as a recipient of an American Cancer Society Educational Stipend for its MSW internship program.

In the period immediately prior to my acceptance of the Virginia directorship, the department also assumed a major leading role in a unique $550,000 grant proposal to enhance patient care services and social work education in the area of child abuse intervention. Collaborating with the OHSU Department of Pediatrics, Rosenfeld Center on the Study of Child Abuse and Neglect, Doernbecher Childrens' Foundation, and Portland State University Graduate School of Social Work, the social work department proposed to fund a specialized physician/social worker child abuse assessment team, establish a computer based, centralized registry of patient cases available to all hospitals, police and the courts, initiate a multidimensional MSW internship program affording both community social service agency and hospital based child abuse intervention experiences, develop intervention training information and create a major forum in which community medical, law enforcement, social work and judicial representatives worked together on a community response to this form of domestic violence.

These large scale collaborative efforts occurred at a time when many facilities, including OHSU, were considering overall downsizing and reconfiguration of services, with potentially negative impacts on patient care departments. As suggested by Rosenberg and Weissman (1984), by maintaining high visibility through creative responses to both patients' needs for services and the hospital's need for financial viability, our intent was to not only provide excellence in patient care but to enhance the profession's organizational posturing and potential for survival in an increasingly turbulent time.

KNOWLEDGE FOR LEADERSHIP

The role of social work services director in a health care setting offers an exceptionally challenging leadership opportunity within the profession. The stimulation is derived from a sophisticated practice environment, caliber of one's colleagues and their professional expectations, complexity of issues with life/death implications confronting department personnel on a daily basis, demands to achieve practice excellence with maximum effectiveness and efficiency and the genuine sense of assisting those in need.

The health care environment expects sensitivity, compassion and professional caring for those in medically compromised situations. At the same time, it has evolved into no less than a rigorous business expressed in terms of revenues, expenses, deductables, operating costs and margins (Lindorff, 1992; Starr, 1982). While using advanced technologies to affect the quality of patients' and families' lives, it is an enterprise increasingly preoccupied not just with patient, but organizational survival, including maximized profitability and investor returns. The problems and impacts of conducting health saving activities as a business enterprise are well documented (Bogdanich, 1991; Ortiz and Bassoff, 1988) and ethically taxing.

To function effectively in an environment increasingly driven by the economics of "managed competition," social work directors must thoroughly understand the tenets and contributions of our profession, maintain a sensitivity to professional ethics and individual health care "consumer" rights and exercise competent, insightful business judgment. As Katz (1978) suggested, leaders must combine technical practice knowledge and a focus on individual and family psychosocial needs, with the ability to keenly detect creative program planning opportunities in a fast paced, competitive, complex organizational structure. To move the department forward, the director must be capable of meshing the goals of department advocacy and the goals of the medical center (Rosenberg, 1987). It is up to the director to have a sense of self-confidence as well as communicate a sense of belief in others' capacities, reward program initiative, encourage creativity and have a love of adventure (Rosenberg, 1987).

Success in this position evolves from a combination of education, professional experience and personality characteristics. The primary responsibilities of the director are to identify patient and institutional needs, initiate appropriate programatic responses, cultivate an environment of social work practice excellence and maintain leadership of sustained effective and efficient operations. To advance social work initiatives where social services are not the primary agenda or there are conflicting priorities, directors must possess a passion for excellence, a sense of optimism, a willingness to persist in the face of formidable challenges, and perhaps most importantly, a sense of vision (Peters and Austin, 1985). Professional drive, administrative competence, personal sensitivity, timing and collaborative skill must be focused and applied in a contemporary practice framework (Peters, 1987; Peters and Austin, 1985; Peters and Waterman, 1982). The intent is to pursue Nacman's (1984) goal of shaping the environment such that social work not only responds to opportunities, but creates its own opportunities. Given the extent and rapidity of contemporary changes, we have the prospect of potentially unparalleled opportunities for social work practice. To recognize and develop those opportunities, however, demands our highest levels of concentration, confidence and initiative.

In my instance, I found that grounding in social work values and skills sensitized me to broad social needs and individual psychodynamics as well as the potentialities of social work as a creative response to those needs. At the same time, graduate education and teaching experiences in business administration substantively contributed to my understanding of organizational design, planning, budgeting, personnel and operations management. Similar preparation is strongly recommended as a basis for understanding the business context in which healthcare social work must be practiced. Progressive experiences in both direct practice and administration combined with a system's theory framework from social work enhanced my ability to assess situations and conceptualize responses that recognized patient, professional and institutional needs. While my management perspective was drawn from the sum of my career experiences and education, my health care experiences, particularly in acute practice settings, have proven most valuable. As a result, my recommendation to those contemplating health care management careers is to maximize their experience in both direct practice and management by making the earliest possible selection of that practice arena. Every opportunity should be taken to develop and maintain professional relationships with other directorate level social workers, capitalizing in particular on the Society for Social Work Administrators in Health Care. Committee and officer appointments, coupled with conference and Chapter meeting attendance contributes to an education, network of friendships and professional revitalization literally without equal. These benefits prove invaluable as administrative positions increasingly require complex, rapid decision making, including determinations that may not prove popular in all quarters. The rewards of these positions can be significant, however, and the fact that health and health care remain primary domestic concerns in our country suggests that the need for competent, energetic and dynamic social work health care leaders will continue well into the future.

REFERENCES

Bagdanich, W. (1991). *The Great White Lie: How America's Hospitals Betray Our Trust and Endanger Our Lives.* New York: Simon and Schuster.

Berkman, B. and Carlton, T.O. (Eds.) (1985). *The Development of Health Social Work Curricula: Patterns and Processes in Three Programs of Social Work Education.* Boston: Massachusetts General Hospital Institute of Health Professions.

Bogo, Marion and Taylor, Imogen. (1990). A practicum curriculum in a health specialization: a framework for hospitals. *Journal of Social Work Education,* 26, 1, 76-86.

Holosio, M.J. and Taylor, P.A. (Eds). (1989). *Social work practice in health care settings.* Toronto: Canadian Scholars' Press.

Katz, R.L. (1978). Skills of an effective administrator. In *Paths Toward Personal Progress: Leaders Are Made, Not Born.* Boston: Harvard Business Review.

Lindorff, D. (1992). *Marketplace Medicine: The Rise of the For-Profit Hospital Chain.* New York: Bantam Books/Doubleday/Dell.

Maricle, R.A., Hosenpud, J.D., Norman, D., Woodbury, A., Pantley, G.A., Cobanoglu, A.M. and Starr, A. (1989). Depression in patients being evaluated for heart transplantation. *General Hospital Psychiatry, 11,* 418-424.

Marshack, Elaine, Davidson, K. and Mizrahi, T. (1988). Preparation of social workers for a changing healthcare environment. *Health and Social Work, 13,* 3, 226-233.

Nacman, M. (1984). Reflections of a social work administrator on the opportunities of crisis. In Laurie, A. and Rosenberg, G. (Eds.), *Social Work Administration in Health Care.* New York: Haworth Press, Inc.

Neely, K. and Spitzer, W. (1993). A model for a statewide critical incident stress (CIS) debriefing program for emergency service personnel. Accepted for publication in the *Journal of Prehospital and Disaster Medicine.*

Ortiz, E.T. and Bassoff, B.Z. (1988). Proprietary hospital social work. *Health and Social Work, 13,* 2 (Spring), 114-121.

Paris, W., Woodbury, A., Thompson, S., Levick, M., Nothegger, S., Hutkin-Slade, L., Arbuckle, P. and Cooper, D.K.C. (1992). Social rehabiliation and return to work after cardiac transplantation–a multicenter survey. *Transplantation, 53,* 2 (February), 433-438.

Peters, T. and Austin, N. (1985). *A Passion for Excellence: The Leadership Difference.* New York: Random House, Inc.

Peters, T.J. and Waterman, R.H. (1982). *In Search of Excellence.* New York: Harper and Row, Inc.

Peters, Tom. (1987). *Thriving on Chaos: Handbook for a Management Revolution.* New York: Harper and Row.

Robinovitch, A.E. and Nash, K.B. (1983). Issues for hospitals in educating social work students for social work practice in health care settings. *Social Work in Health Care, 9,* 2, 97-105.

Rosenberg, G. (1987). The social worker as manager in health care settings: an experiential view. *Social Work in Health Care, 12,* 3 (Spring), 71-84.

Rosenberg, G. and Weissman, A. (1984). Marketing social services in health care facilities. In A. Lurie and G. Rosenberg (Eds.), *Social Work Administration in Health Care.* New York: The Haworth Press, Inc.

Spitzer, W. and Kuykendall, R. (1994). Social work delivery of hospital based financial assistance services. *Health and Social Work, 19,* 4, 295-297.

Spitzer, W. and Nash, K. (1995). Educational preparation for contemporary health care social work practice. Accepted for publication–*Social Work in Health Care.*

Spitzer, W. and Burke, L. (1993). A critical stress debriefing program for hospital based health care personnel. *Health and Social Work, 18,* 2, 149-56.

Spitzer, W. and Neely, K. (1992). Critical incident stress: the role of hospital-based social work in developing a statewide intervention system for first responders delivering emergency services. *Social Work in Health Care, 18,* 1, 39-58.

Spitzer, W. (1990). Oregon–an example of interorganizational alliance building for graduate social work health care education. *Social Work Administration, 16,* 3, 24-30.

Starr, P. (1982). *The Social Transformation of American Medicine.* New York: Basic Books, Inc.

Preliminary Thoughts on Sustaining Central Social Work Departments

Gary Rosenberg, PhD
Andrew Weissman, DSW

In this section we briefly outline the major changes occurring in health care, particularly in the management of the for-profit business world, and the implications for social work departments in health care.

"The U.S. is witnessing the most drastic industry reorganization since the 19th century–the corporate take over of American health care. Giant health systems have been created, formed not by their own desires, but in the crucible of employer and insurer demands for lower costs and by a government unable to legislate health reform"(The Governance Committee, 1993).

Businesses and governmental agencies that pay for the cost of health care have organized in order to force the insured population to use specific health care providers. They have exchanged the freedom of choice for patients with lower costs for those paying the bill.

Given the changing economic nature of the health care delivery system, we can point to four characteristics which will help shape the way the systems operate:

1. The system will be vertically integrated. From preventive services, wellness programs and health education, through primary care, secondary, and acute care to long term care: all services will be handled through one unified system.

[Haworth co-indexing entry note]: "Preliminary Thoughts on Sustaining Central Social Work Departments." Rosenberg, Gary, and Andrew Weissman. Co-published simultaneously in *Social Work in Health Care* (The Haworth Press, Inc.) Vol. 20, No. 4, 1995, pp. 111-116; and: *Social Work Leadership in Healthcare: Directors' Perspectives* (ed: Gary Rosenberg, and Andrew Weissman), The Haworth Press, Inc., 1995, pp. 111-116. Multiple copies of this article/chapter may be purchased from The Haworth Document Delivery Center [1-800-3-HAWORTH; 9:00 a.m. - 5:00 p.m. (EST)].

2. Regional system coverage will replace local catchment areas as the dominant form of targeting patients resulting in a wide geographic area of people being served.
3. Payment by capitation. The health care system will share the risks and possible rewards and will be paid a flat fee per "covered life."
4. Costs will be lower; 15% to 20% below the present non managed care market prices.

In order to increase the scope of health care services while at the same time decreasing the costs of health care, this new health care delivery system will require the redeployment of resources and people:

1. From inpatient acute care to outpatient care.
2. From the current specialist settings to primary care programs.
3. From tertiary care to early diagnosis and prevention.

The major changes occurring in the organization of health care delivery are also affected by restructuring of the system itself.

Most health care systems are moving to a flatter, more horizontal organizational structure out of economic necessity. Just as the commercial for-profit industries have downsized and streamlined as much as they can, so will the health care systems. But more must be done for the system to remain competitive. Simply laying off people does not achieve organizational goals. We have to change the way the work is done, change the processes, and drive out the unnecessary work or it will reappear overnight. Our staffs can't keep doing more with less. We need to identify and eliminate the superfluous work (Campy, 1995).

The central idea, taken from the business world, is to organize around core processes, rather than functions; to get everyone focused on the business as a system. A system in this approach, needs to be seamless, uncluttered with boundaries among departments where discontinuities can occur, where difficult and unnecessary work processes can appear (Bergman, 1994).

These fiscal concerns and drive for higher levels of productivity have led to an increasing number of hospitals' restructuring, both by expanding into health care systems and by flattening administrative structures of differing parts of the health care system.

With the health care system restructuring, professional groups have had to define and justify themselves to the health system administration and each other. The issue of which professional boundaries to maintain in this current environment has become extremely problematic.

The professions state that practice expertise is specific and unique to each health care discipline, and therefore organizations need a centralized administrative structure. Health care system managers want and need multiple cross-trained staff to remove boundaries, as one way to improve patient care and reduce costs (Ford and Randolph, 1992; Dimond, 1993; Globeman and Bogo, 1995). In order to bridge these divergent perspectives we need to develop structural models that fit the values and concerns of these newly designed health care systems with social work's professional goals.

How does a profession maintain and control standards for quality professional practice, staff education, teaching and research, and the development of innovative programs of care in these new health care systems?

The challenge for social work is to develop appropriate structures that address the need to be professionals, researchers, and focuses on practice innovation and change.

If we assume that the health care system will be a flat organization, driven by the product owners and managers (medical programs and procedures), what role should a central department play?

A centralized social work department's goal is to be flexible, able to respond immediately to emerging patient care needs, medical program teams needs, community needs, and health care system needs. Therefore, we think our central role should be to the community—to provide services to the underserved, the disenfranchised, the chronically ill, those who, out of ignorance and where our current structures foster abuse, utilize the most expensive care in an inappropriate manner. We need to help implement programs that provide the right mix of health care services at the right time. Programs that aim at prevention, health promotion, wellness, and continuity and that encompass community outreach to the vulnerable populations need to be developed and implemented. To accomplish these goals we should be closely tied to primary care health care systems (Simmons, 1994; Rosenberg, 1994).

Our social work role needs to focus on the environmental assaults that are affecting patients served by our health care system. Lead, asbestos, housing all impact the health care and the costs of health care in the populations we serve.

We need to meet the needs of the health care system by defining a role to innovate, experiment, create and–by means of grants–to produce creative programs that forward the mission of the health care system where we work.

We need, through strong quality assurance programs, to be able to guarantee our patients, the health care system, and all of the regulatory agencies of the high quality and high standards of our services.

We also need to provide our professional staff with quality continuing education courses and to play a significant role in training students.

To achieve the above mentioned role, social could operate in at least 5 domains.

We need to:

1. Create health education and health promotion programs to aid in health maintenance and disease prevention in defined populations.
2. Develop screening instruments for use in primary care. Instruments can be used to provide early intervention for those who are at high risk for adverse psychosocial problems related to health, for those who need family assistance, or for those who need other resource services. We need to help identify potential people who, without timely intervention, use an inordinate amount of health care system resources (e.g., the populations that abuse alcohol, cigarettes, and drugs).
3. Provide psychosocial services to the growing population of chronically ill people including those with behavioral health problems.
4. Provide services to the elderly and those who support them.
5. Link social work agencies to the health care system to avoid the duplication of services within a community.

To develop these identified roles and operate more successfully in the specified domains the skills and leadership steps (Legnini, 1994), outlined in the previous chapters that may be required of social work directors in this environment are:

1. To be able to accurately read the environment of your community and of your health care system.
2. To re-engineer your own department (before it is done for you). Where possible compress layers of management; hasten the move from inpatient focus to outpatient locus by the judicious assignment of staff social workers.
3. Maintain your strengths. Start with those medical programs that value social work services, where you are recognized, appreciated and effective.
4. Create new models of care; experiment, innovate, and write grants to support new service ideas.
5. Use relationships with community groups to develop partnerships that create responsive health programs based on social epidemiologic information.

We do not believe one model or one type of social work director is best. We do believe that attention to the specific components we have identified is necessary to enable a central social work department to continue to thrive. It is necessary but not sufficient as these areas must be supplemented based on the individual system where social work is practiced.

We hope and believe that the articles included in this issue will help our current and future social work leaders in health care maintain and expand our traditional values and practice commitments.

REFERENCES

Bergman, Rhonda, (1995), Reengineering health care, *Hospitals and Health Networks*, February 5, 28-36.
Campy, James S. (1995), *Reengineering Management*, New York: Harper Business.
Dimond, Margaret, (1993), Cross functional management: Strategies for changing times, *Social Work Administration, 19* (4) 1-12.
Ford, R.C. and Randolph W.A. (1992), Cross functional structures: A review and integration of matrix organization and project management. *Journal of Management, 18* (2) 267-294.

Globeman, J. and Bogo, M. (1995), Social Work and the New Integrative Hospi-
tal. *Social Work in Health Care, 21* (3), in press.
The Governance Committee, (1993), *Vision of the future*, The Advisory Board,
Washington, D.C.
Legnini, M.W., (1994), Developing leaders vs. training administrators in the
health services, *American Journal of Public Health, 84 (10)* 1569-1572.
Rosenberg Gary, (1994), Social work, the family and the community, *Social Work
in Health Care, 20* (1) 7-20.
Simmons June, (1994), Community based care: The new health social work
paradigm. *Social Work in Health Care, 20* (1) 35-46.

For Product Safety Concerns and Information please contact our EU
representative GPSR@taylorandfrancis.com Taylor & Francis Verlag GmbH,
Kaufingerstraße 24, 80331 München, Germany

Printed and bound by CPI Group (UK) Ltd, Croydon, CR0 4YY
08/05/2025
01864355-0002